You're Retiring to Ecuador? Are You Loco?

You're Retiring to Ecuador? Are You Loco?

A direct quote from family, friends,
and especially Ecuadorians in Chicago

by Wayne Robert Hanson
A Chicago Expat in Ecuador

You're Retiring to Ecuador? Are You Loco?

Windy City Publishers
2118 Plum Grove Road, #349
Rolling Meadows, IL 60008
www.windycitypublishers.com

Published in the United States of America

ISBN:
978-1-941478-16-5

Library of Congress Control Number:
2015957029

WINDY CITY PUBLISHERS
CHICAGO

To Estée

To Sherry, Erich, Graham, and Lily

To Ecuador,
our new and permanent home
(unless we get kicked out)

Disclaimer

The information contained in this book does not constitute a travel guide, nor is it intended to be a guide to the ins and outs of retiring to Ecuador. Myriad books cover those subjects. It does not contain advice that any sane person should use. However, if you are not sane, then please do not come to Ecuador. We seem to be full up with less-than-sane people flooding into the seaports and buzzing into the airports of this small country. My wife, Estée, and I may be among them. After you read this book, you can make the call.

Immigration rules change constantly in Ecuador, as do the rules and regulations for moving animals, possessions, and funds to Ecuador from the United States or any other country. If you are considering retiring to Ecuador, you may find that from the time you start your extensive research (an absolute requirement) to the time you actually get serious about retiring to Ecuador, the rules have changed, and they may change again after that. Do your homework. Don't let the dog eat it.

You won't find a chapter on the religions of Ecuador in this book. Around ninety-five percent of Ecuadorians are Catholic or sort-of Catholic. I really do not want ninety-five percent—or even sort-of ninety-five percent—of the people of my new country angry with me. Likewise, I have declined to discuss politics, which is very similar to religion in the passion it engenders. I really want to stay in Ecuador. It is a lot like Christmas dinner with relatives: don't mention religion or politics and things will go smoothly. Okay, probably not, but things will likely go better.

The impetus to write this book came from a series of incidents outlined in the chapter "The Premature Death Certificate: Enough Said." After living through the events described in that chapter, I started keeping a journal of our experiences in Ecuador. The book emanated from that journal. All the events in this book are real simply because I cannot make this stuff up. All of the people in the book are real, and I have almost always used their real names. To stay out of court, I have disguised the names of those few who might take umbrage with the way I treated them (no matter how much they deserved it).

Despite all the help, the content of this book, in its entirety, is my responsibility—unless you are planning to sue me, then it is clearly someone else's responsibility, and I can prove it in court.

contents

"At certain periods it becomes the dearest ambition of a man
to keep a faithful record of his performances in a book;
and he dashes at this work with an enthusiasm that imposes on him
the notion that keeping a journal is the veriest pastime in the world,
and the pleasantest. But if he only lives twenty-one days,
he will find out that only those rare natures that are made up of pluck, endur-
ance, devotion to duty for duty's sake, and invincible determination
may hope to venture upon so tremendous an enterprise as the
keeping of a journal and not sustain a shameful defeat."

From *The Innocents Abroad* by Mark Twain

chapter 1

Retirement:
You're Retiring Where? No Really, Where?

Estée and I woke up on a Sunday morning in 2004, looked at one another, and simultaneously said, "Let's retire. Where should we go? Oh, yes, let's retire to Ecuador! By the way, where is Ecuador? Is that a city or a country? Or is it an island?" That's not what really happened, but that is what nearly all of our friends and acquaintances seemed to believe. While we are not averse to being whimsical at times, we do not approach a decision of that gravity with whimsy. While it might make a nice narrative, the real story is quite different.

When Estée and I met in Chicago and got married, some of our first conversations had to do with where we wanted to retire. These conversations usually took place from November through March and sometimes into April. Anyone who has lived in Chicago or a similar climate from November through early April will understand.

The thought of retiring can cause paroxysms in many people. There are so many issues and questions to consider. Answers to those questions are different, but generally equally difficult, for everyone. Is there enough money in the bank to retire? What will I do in retirement? Do I have hobbies that will keep my interest and sustain me for years to come? Can I stand living with my significant other 24/7? Does my significant other even want to retire at this point? What about health issues? Where should I retire? Near our kids—even though they might leave any time and take the grandkids with them? What will I do if my spouse dies before me? Would I even consider retiring in a

1

foreign land? Retirement for many people is a terrifying prospect, for many good reasons.

While retirement was a long way off, we knew that we would not retire in Chicago, even though both of us love the city. The mayors Daley, father and son, both had profound effects on the city over many years. (There were a couple of mayors in between, but memories of them are less sanguine.) During most of the time we lived there, Chicago was under the guidance of Mayor Richard M. Daley—Richey to his friends. During his twenty-two-year tenure, Chicago blossomed into a world-class city that any resident would be proud to live in and brag about.

We lived in the first suburb west of Chicago, called Oak Park, where Hemingway was born and Frank Lloyd Wright had one of his studios. Hemingway referred to Oak Park as a suburb of wide lawns and narrow minds. Frank Lloyd Wright built over forty beautiful and unique homes in Oak Park, all with wide lawns. We did not have a Frank Lloyd Wright home. We did not even have a wide lawn, so I took some courage in the belief that I might possibly have a wide mind.

I moved to Oak Park in 1978, just in time for the famous winter of '78–'79. All you have to say to anyone who was near Chicago during that time is "the bad winter," and they will say "ah, the winter of '78–'79." The area was hit with three consecutive massive blizzards, each worse than the previous one. There was no time to dig out of the first storm, let alone the subsequent two.

Following the third storm, the temperatures plummeted to dangerous levels so you could not be outside for more than a minute or two before tender parts of your body began to freeze and crack as a prelude to falling off. The snow was so deep that the heads of the parking meters were completely covered. The Village of Oak Park actually had city workers and extra part-time employees dig down to uncover the heads of the meters. The Oak Park traffic police ticketed stranded cars whose owners did not feed the meters. To feed the meters from the buried sidewalks, one had to get on one's hands and knees, or even lay on the snow, and reach down to put multiple quarters in the meter. Occasionally an Oak Park traffic policeman or policewoman would be lying on the snow to read the meter as the owner would be trying to feed the meter. This was a dangerous situation, and after several of these encounters, the chief of the

Oak Park Traffic Division decided that the draconian measures being practiced by the Traffic Division could be delayed until the snow had been cleared, or at least practiced when the owners were not present.

Driving was out of the question, so both Estée and I took public transportation—something we wanted to do anyway, but not under those circumstances. To get to work at Rush-Presbyterian St. Luke's Medical Center where I was an assistant professor and head of research in the department of radiation oncology, I had to take a bus to the El (for elevated) train stop, and then the El to the medical center stop, west of the city. At the end of the day, the trip was reversed. During and after the triple storms, commuting was an adventure.

Estée took a different El train that deposited her within a few steps of the beauty salon she owned called Estée Hanson Coiffures in the heart of Chicago. The fact that she was right downtown gave her a huge commuter advantage, since she could be one of the first passengers to board the train on her way back home to Oak Park.

One fateful afternoon after the third blizzard, at about 5:30, I went to the medical center stop to catch the westbound train for home. I marched up and down the platform to try to keep warm. I was marching up and down the platform with about fifty other people, and it brought back memories of army basic training at Fort Leonard Wood, Missouri, eight years before. I considered calling out "your left, your left, your left-right-left" in the southern drawl that my drill sergeant used, but I resisted. The bad memories of the Vietnam War were still fresh for a lot of people in the late seventies.

The marching did absolutely no good. I was freezing. Everyone was straining to see if the headlights of the westbound train were visible. There was no train. The fear was that if you gave up and walked the ten minutes back to the nearest warm building, you would miss your ride. I gave up, marched the requisite ten minutes, and spent precious time warming up. Then it was back to the platform to join the now nearly one hundred soldiers marching up and down the platform. My gamble had paid off, though, and I had not missed the train.

Excitement rippled throughout the gathering on the platform as someone thought he saw the headlights of the westbound train above the tracks. It was a feeling of anticipation similar to the one I had at a concert waiting for Elton

John to take the stage. (In that case, it turned out that he was actually on stage, but I was so far away out on a lawn with poles and trees in my line of view that I could not make out his short, stocky figure prancing around the piano.)

And yes, there they were, headlights moving westbound at two miles an hour. Like Elton John at the concert, the headlights looked miles away, so I thought we would all be dead, frozen on the platform like the unlucky German troops surrounding Stalingrad in WWII. We would be found with our frozen legs and arms in different directions with peaceful expressions of anticipation on our faces. Perhaps our surviving relatives could get Elton John to play at our mass funeral. Like the gravity of a black hole, we collectively drew the headlights toward us, and with sighs of relief, we watched as the train painfully pulled into the station.

What happened next nearly brought war to the platform. The frozen metal of the train car doors creaked and groaned as they slowly slid open, emitting a cloud of collected breath from the passengers within. The huge size of the cloud suggested that it had been formed from a lot of breath, and it was. Not only breath emerged; passengers near each door were involuntarily disgorged from the train from the pressure of the packed humanity within. A tin of sardines had more free space than that train. The surprised expressions on the faces of the disgorged passengers coming from the office buildings, banks, and shops of downtown Chicago quickly turned to fear. Their suspicious and darting eyes were matched by the expressions of fear on the faces of the nearly frozen medical center soldiers on the platform. Who was going to have the privilege of being the next sardine in the train car?

The events that followed could not really be described as pushing and shoving. It was more like clawing, tripping, yelling and shouting, jabbing, swearing, and otherwise acting like English thugs at a soccer match in Berlin. I am not good in those situations, so I clutched my briefcase and trudged back to the warmth of the medical center. This time I had a hot cup of coffee, called home, and gave Estée a briefing on how extraordinarily rude some people can be.

A full forty-five minutes went by, and I thought that surely by now the number of people coming from the city would have diminished and I could zip home to a glass of red wine, a hot meal, and the warmth of a fire to prepare for the same ordeal the next day. I marched back to the train stop to find nearly one hundred more people waiting—not a good sign. I recognized some from forty-five minutes ago, which was a terrible sign.

Everyone knew the drill by now. There were scouts who looked for the headlights and there were troops who marched up and down the platform to keep warm. After what seemed like hours but was only a few minutes, another train slowly crept into the station. Lady Luck was on my side this time, because with my marching, I was inadvertently positioned near a door when it creaked open. A huge cloud of breath emerged and some human sardines spurted out of the doorway, pushed by their fellow sardines in the train. In the ensuing scrum to push others aside to get onto the train, I was carried into the doorway and onto the train without actually taking a step.

While that was quite amazing, what I found in the train was even more astonishing. It was packed so tightly that where any body part was at that moment, it remained for the duration of the ride. My left hand gripped the handle of my soft briefcase, which was pressed painfully into my left leg. I could feel the metal clasps on the side of the leather case pushing into my thigh. As I was being transported into the train car, I had instinctively put my right hand up toward my chest in a defensive stance, and there it stayed. More clawing, tripping, yelling and shouting, jabbing, and swearing was going on behind me; but miraculously, I was on the El train, and I was on my way home.

The train pulled slowly away from the din of verbal disappointment and outright abuse that arose from the medical center stop and settled into a bumpy to-and-fro motion that, on a normal ride, can lull one to sleep. This was not a normal ride. As soon as my mind cleared and I realized that I had made it onto a train that was only slightly warmer than the platform, I became aware of just how packed together everyone was. That slightly greater warmth came from body heat, which carried with it, shall we be kind and say, "a certain musky odor." I could not move at all—not a foot, not a hand, nothing. Only my head could rotate. Like some strange physical law, everything else had to remain exactly where it was in space.

After a short time, I realized that my right hand was touching something quite soft and warm. Gravity was pulling my hand slowly down into more soft-ness and warmth. Living in a big city in America, one learns either quickly or harshly that eye contact in public should be avoided under almost all circumstances. Everyone in that packed train was either looking up at the ceiling, at the station maps displayed at intervals on the walls of the train, or, if possible, out a window. There was no eye contact. I decided that it might be important to break that rule and have a look downward at what was so soft and warm. I looked down toward where my right hand was disappearing, and into the gaze of a short, sixty-something-year-old obese woman with long, red-dyed hair, dark eyes, and jowls that shook with the rhythm of the train. We were front to front, and from the feel of her whole body, which was pressed oh-so-tightly into mine, I could tell that she easily outweighed me even though she was about 5 ft. 2 in. compared to my six-foot, not-so-small frame.

My heavy-duty Eddie Bauer goose-down parka, which was advertised to keep me warm to negative twenty degrees, was not helping insulate me from that body. My right hand was slowly sinking in between her voluminous soft and warm breasts. The motion of the train caused a jiggling that could, under other circumstances, be titillating, but in this particular circumstance caused sheer panic within my very soul. All I could think of was the tawdry novels that my religious mother tried to protect me from in my adolescence, the ones that contained the phrase "as his hand slowly sank between her..." I tried to extricate the offending hand, fearing that it would be the cause of far-greater consequences down the tracks. I absolutely could not move. The only thing I could do was to apologize, so I weakly said, "Sorry about this." Her dark-brown eyes met my blue eyes, and I received a wide smile without a tooth to be seen.

In the ensuing eleven years that I worked at the medical center, I took the train perhaps five more times. I did not make eye contact with anyone ever again, and I always wondered if she would recognize me if she saw me, and what she would do to me—or for me—if she did. I shudder to this day.

Although no winter in Chicago since then has risen to the level of discomfort that people suffered during the infamous winter of '78–'79, it was clear after that winter that Estée and I would not be retiring in the Midwest or anywhere north of there. At that time, there was no great rush to make a decision; we had years before we had to get serious about retirement. Occasionally, however, I did consult older friends and colleagues about their thoughts on retiring.

On one such occasion, Estée and I were visiting a friend and colleague, Dr. John Ainsworth, one of my favorite mentors during my professional training. He and his wife, Caroline, lived in Bethesda, Maryland, and were considering retirement in a few years. John was the civilian director of a military laboratory in Bethesda where the military director held sway over operations. The military position was rotated every four years, and each service had its turn, so one four-year span saw a director from the army, followed by the navy, then the air force. Some military directors were great and some were, well, not so great. During the not-so-great years, John would go to Costco and buy the largest tub of Vaseline he could find and keep it in his deep, left-bottom drawer. When a not-so-good military director would enter his office, he would retrieve the vat of Vaseline, plop it on top of his desk, and begin difficult conversations with the request to "please use the Vaseline, and please be gentle." I adopted this practice with some of my bosses during the years, and it got me through some bad times; however, I had some bosses for whom there was simply not enough Vaseline in the world.

John and his wife took us to Rock Creek Park, which had many beautiful nooks and crannies in which to wander around. During the wandering, I asked John if he thought a lot about retiring. He replied, "Only when I am awake; at night, I dream about it." Perhaps it was after that comment that Estée and I started to get more serious about the prospect.

One of the hobbies Estée and I share is SCUBA diving, so we let our minds wander when we were diving at locations like Belize, Honduras, Costa Rica, Venezuela, Grand Cayman Islands, and the Turks and Caicos Islands. One location in particular struck us as a great possibility for a retirement destination. We fell in love with Ecuador.

My introduction to Ecuador years before was less than favorable. I was ten years old, sitting captive in the Nashua Bible Church in rural Iowa. Nashua was a typical dying farm town in the Midwest with a population of about eighteen hundred people. When I left seven years later, it was populated with about thirteen hundred people and falling. Nashua is near the fictitious town featured in the book and movie *A Thousand Acres*.

Nashua was, and I am sure still is, a great town in which to grow up, but once you graduated from high school, there was little to do to make a living other than working on the family farm. My family did not have one. My parents were religious people, especially my mother, who insisted that my older brother and I attend Sunday school, then the regular Sunday service, then, later that night, the Sunday evening service. To top it off, we were dragged on most Wednesdays to an evening prayer meeting. All these church services proved to me beyond any doubt that Einstein was correct: time is relative, and under some circumstances, time stops.

On a Sunday in 1956 during the regular service, Pastor Max Ward announced that a special collection was to be taken to help the spouses and children of five missionary men who had been brutally slaughtered in the jungles of Ecuador by members of the Waorani tribe. I had never heard of Ecuador, let alone the Waorani tribe. The phrase "brutally slaughtered" sounded serious—especially to a ten-year-old—so I had a lot of questions, but my parents hushed me. An article in the *Des Moines Register* that provided more details of the brutal slaughter was read from the pulpit the next Sunday, so the news stayed around for quite a while, especially for me.

The thoughts and unanswered questions I had as a ten-year-old came back to me as American Airlines flight 932 began its decent into Quito, Ecuador, in 1995, nearly forty years after the brutal slaughter. I really did not know what to expect, but I thought that surely things had changed and we SCUBA-diving tourists would not be set upon and brutally slaughtered by the Waorani tribe. Surely Bruce, our group leader and owner of a dive shop in Chicago's Villa Park, had done his research before arranging the trip to avoid such a headline event. Still, I envisioned my colleagues reading the short two paragraphs on page ten of the *Chicago Tribune* with the phrases "brutally slaughtered" and "if only they had planned better." I let the other passengers disembark first just in case. There was not a Waorani tribesman to be seen.

Quito was a modern city of about one-and-a-half million people, although there had not been a census for a long time. After a night listening to the "barking dogs of Quito" (a direct quote from an Ecuador guide book which implored travelers to bring industrial earplugs and that I read *after* the trip), we took off for the Galapagos Islands for two great weeks of diving and sightseeing. At the end of the dive trip, we spent a few days north of Quito. We found the people of Ecuador to be fascinating and the valley- and mountainscapes stunningly beautiful.

Our next trip to Ecuador was in order to see orchids in their wild habitat. This is when we met Pepe and Ingrid Portilla, the owners of Ecuagenera, an orchid company headquartered in Gualaceo, about thirty-five kilometers east of Cuenca. After many discussions with Pepe and Ingrid, a great deal of encouragement from them, and the promise of help getting settled, we decided to do our "due diligence" and get serious about retiring to Ecuador. Let the fun begin!

Our decision to retire to Ecuador was met with what could politely be described as a mixed reaction. Most of the mixture was amused disbelief, folded in with incredulity and a touch of anger by some, but mostly disbelief. "Are you out of your minds?" was a frequently voiced sentiment. "Are they out of their minds?" was the phrase used among our family, friends, colleagues, and clients. Our Latino friends used the term *loco*. Our good friends and neighbors, Bill and Bob, simply would not accept our decision. One friend and colleague, a professor at the University of Chicago, was convinced that he would see pictures in the paper of us in a pot of boiling oil as we were featured on the menu of the local tribe eatery. Our daughter sputtered when we announced what we were planning. Her first thoughts were of abandonment, forgetting that she and her husband were considering moving from the Chicago area, first to the West Coast, then to the East Coast. It had not occurred to her that *we* could leave. After all, we were the home nest and she was the bird free to fly off and set up her nest somewhere else. She had no qualms about her moving but a lot of qualms about our plans. When our plans were announced to my mother, she calmly asked, "Do you plan to be buried there?" On the list of the hundreds of questions I expected from her, that was not even on the list.

Estée's clients at her beauty salon had a more honest and selfish reaction. The most frequent comment was, "But what will I do about my hair? Why are you doing this to me?" I know that a great hairdresser is one of the more important people in one's life, but neither Estée nor I were prepared for the reactions. The parking valets, who were Ecuadorians and who worked in front of Estee's shop, were particularly vexed. They had spent huge amounts of money and many long months or years making their way from Ecuador to Chicago. And now, two gringos are spending huge amounts of money and time to go to Ecuador. The irony was not lost on them as they asked, "Are you loco?" In many respects, the reactions of our family, friends, colleagues, and clients were a great compliment. Indifference would have been devastating.

Now it was time to make our lists of pros and cons—to refine them, to do research on every aspect we could think of, and to do everything we could to make certain that we would not end up in a pot of boiling oil, either figuratively or literally. The pro list was extensive and included climate—meaning the lack of Chicago winters. Cost of living was a positive, especially considering property taxes that were costing us about $14,000 a year in Oak Park. The excitement factor was very high on the pro list as well. I was anxious to pursue my hobby of photography, and there was so much to pursue.

The con list was much shorter, but it was headed by one very important item: missing our family and friends. We extracted promises from everyone we could that they would visit, but we knew that for one reason or another, we would see most of our friends very infrequently, if at all, from the time we left. That was hard to contemplate. Another con on our list was the language barrier, especially for me.

Estée has a gift for languages. Spanish would become her sixth language, discounting the Latin she had in Romania. Her first encounter with the need to speak another language occurred when she was seven years old. Estée was born in Transylvania, about forty kilometers from the ruins of Vlad the Impaler's (Count Dracula's) castle. Her parents were Hungarian, but history played some nasty tricks on them, as history is prone to do, especially in that part of the world. After WWII, Estée's parents went to sleep in Hungary and woke up in Romania, complements of Russia. Transylvania was a "gift" to Romania for their cooperation with Russia during the war.

At seven years old, Estée started school and was taught only in Romanian, which she did not speak or understand. She wandered around school smiling at the teachers and playing. After a short time, her utopia was shattered by a visit to her parents from the school principal, who told them that their daughter must learn and speak Romanian. There was no other option. Hence, two of the six languages Estée speaks are Hungarian and Romanian. Her other languages are Italian, French, English, and now Spanish.

As for me, the genes for language learning certainly existed in my heritage, or my mother's half of it at least. My mother was Danish, taught high school German, and after studying in Vienna and Heidelberg was mistaken for a Berliner when traveling in Germany. She spent five years in the Philippines and learned Tagalog as well. On the other hand, my father had none of those genes. He had a difficult time in England, although in his defense, understanding Cockney can be a challenge. Through the blessings and curses of the magic of genetics, I got the non-language genes. I suffered through German classes at the university where we translated Faust, but I found that the translation did little by way of assisting me in ordering from a menu in the Black Forest town of Titisee. I had been invited to give a talk at a small medical conference in this remote village with very few restaurant choices.

After several nights, I was tired of Wienerschnitzel and wanted to branch out. I did not know anyone at the conference, so I was eating alone, something I really do not like to do. The non-English-speaking young German waitress was very kind and tried to guide me to something she thought I would like, but I was insistent on one item, thinking that the higher price would provide me with a tasty and tender piece of beef tenderloin or something like it. The waitress used a large number of incomprehensible German words that were not covered in my translation of Faust to explain my culinary decision. I had no idea what she was saying. She disappeared into the kitchen and returned with a whole new set of incomprehensible German words also not covered in Faust. Evidently, Faust never ate in Titisee. On her next trip from the kitchen, I could see a distinct blush on her already rosy cheeks. She glanced around the small dining room to be certain that no one was looking, and raised her hands above her own ears to form large ears over her head. In a hushed but audible voice, she whispered, "Hee haw, hee haw." I was about to order mule meat. In retrospect, I am sorry that I had the Wienerschnitzel again, but at the time, my sense of culinary adventure was rather stifled.

There were many more items on both the pro and the con list, but we went through each of them systematically and convinced ourselves that we could deal with each one. Now it was time to set a timetable and to make a list of things to do. Selling the house (quit laughing), looking for land, and moving were the first major items on top of the list.

chapter 2

Where to Build:
Looking for Land in All the Wrong Places

After we made the decision that Ecuador, in general, and the area around Gualaceo, specifically, was the place we wanted to build our house, we needed to find land. By 2005, Estée and I had been to Gualaceo several times. On each trip, we were shown many parcels of land by friends, relatives of friends, their aunts and uncles, friends of their aunts and uncles, and a stranger named Carlos Jesus.

Along with looking for land with our Ecuadorian friends, we looked for an architect who might be helpful in finding land as well. We needed to find an honest and talented architect to build our dream/retirement home in Ecuador. Pepe, our Ecuadorian friend who promised to help us, recommended an architect whom he claimed was honest. This architect, Pepe assured us, was so honest that if he gave you a brick and said there was an ounce of gold in the middle, there was an ounce of gold in the middle. At today's gold prices, it would be foolish to put it in a brick, but I got Pepe's point. In the end, we'd learn that this architect was more than willing to put lead in your brick, but this is a topic for a later chapter.

At least the architect was helpful during the early stages of our project. People with small to huge plots of land came out of nowhere to sell it to the "rich" gringos. We gave our requirements to the kind people whose duty it was that day to drive us around and show us pieces of land they knew we would fall in love with, and for which they hoped we would pay huge gobs of money.

We were picked up by Santiago (evidently a friend of someone we were supposed to know) and the architect on a Wednesday morning in April of 2005 and set out on a winding road to a hilltop that was for sale. I was riding in the front passenger seat because it was easier for me to get in and out of the car with a left hip that was badly in need of replacement. We pulled to a stop and, with not a little effort, I pushed the passenger-side door open against a cold wind that was just slightly less than gale force. The view was spectacular, provided one could keep one's eyes open in the wind that produced the tears that clouded one's view. We were assured that a beautiful home could be constructed on the hilltop and the price of the land would be far less than it would be in the valley.

I sensed that this was for good reason, as all the other hilltops in our view did not have Spanish-style country homes sitting on them. In fact, there were no adobe homes or pigpens. Even hen houses were out of the question because there would be feathers and chicken parts strewn all through the valley. There were no homes or structures of any kind on any of the hilltops. Not only that, there were no trees, shrubs, bushes, or flowers in which to frolic. There were barely any weeds growing there: only a short, sickly looking grass that could survive in the constantly windswept, cold climate of the high ground.

Estée asked, in her not-so-timid way, what Santiago did not understand regarding our wish to live near a lake, a river, a pond, or even a puddle? His not-so-convincing answer was, "But you can see a river from here." And, indeed, if it had not been for the trees, shrubs, bushes, and flowers growing around Spanish-style houses by the river, you could have seen it. It turned out that a relative of Santiago's owned this land and was in desperate need to unload it on some poor suckers. On that day, at least, we avoided being the suckers.

This general story was repeated many times over many trips to Gualaceo. On one occasion, we were taken by the architect to a plot of land on the Santa Barbara River on the southern outskirts of Gualaceo. At first I was excited because the plot fulfilled many of our requirements. It had the river nearby, trees and other greenery, and plenty of space to build on. Estée and I exchanged hopeful looks as we started down a path to take a closer look near the river.

That was when my right foot sank into the ground and water poured into my tennis shoe. Estée was wearing boots, but by the time I could warn her, she had one foot stuck in the ground and was desperately trying to keep her balance to avoid a mud bath. With help, we extricated ourselves from what was clearly a flood plain. I asked the architect how often the river overflowed its banks and flooded this parcel of land in an average year. One hint that this was not infrequent was the presence of plastic bags and other river debris in the trees over my head. There was a lot of hemming and hawing and equivocating. Finally, a bold answer was formulated. "Not very often; don't worry about it," was the conjured answer. This was the first time we encountered what would soon become a familiar phrase—"don't worry about it." This phrase was to resurface many times during the construction of our house.

On another occasion, the architect took us in his car to a piece of land for sale in a valley near the San Francisco River. Going out of Gualaceo on the eastbound road toward Macas, we turned off onto a grass driveway. There was a small adobe house on the left, a gently sloping cornfield to the right, and the river at the bottom. There were some native Ecuadorian willow trees near the river and a hummingbird drinking from a pink hibiscus tree near the house. Mountains sprang up on all sides of the valley. This was it! It fulfilled nearly every requirement we had in mind. The architect sensed our excitement and explained that he would do the negotiating. If the owner got the idea that we wanted the land, the price would be considerably higher.

The owner and his wife came out toward the car. We were told to stay put and look as Ecuadorian as possible. This was no small feat since I have snow-white hair and blue eyes. I kept my hat on and my eyes closed. The architect got out of the car and tried to keep the owners from seeing us. He explained that he was only modestly interested in the land to buy for an Ecuadorian friend, but there were many other properties for sale that were much more appealing. I was impressed with his approach, the details of which I had to guess at since I did not have a clue what he was saying at the time. The owner correctly surmised that the level of bullshit contained in the conversation was high. His price for about one-and-a-half acres of land was $300,000. He hastened to add that the price included the small crumbling adobe house, which had cable TV, as if somehow Fox News broadcast on cable TV in rural Ecuador would justify the asking price. The architect snorted that the owner should just ask five million and be done with it. The owner instantly came down to $200,000, which was almost as ridiculous. The damage was done. Estée and I were genuinely disappointed. This was the ideal place but it was grossly overpriced.

By this time, we had seen a large number of places, and I began to talk about compromise. If we did not need to live by a lake or even a puddle of water, then there would be many more possibilities. Estée did not give up so easily. She was sure there would be a place for us.

Pepe told us that he thought there was some land for sale across the river from the greenhouses of Ecuagenera. He alerted the architect, who went to scout it out. Sure enough, there was a seven-acre triangular plot of land with not one, but two rivers that formed two sides of the triangle: a small one flowing into a larger one. There were myriad trees lining both rivers and the land sloped upwards toward a road where an access lane could easily be cleared. Flooding was not an issue.

The views on the day we first saw the property were splendid and verdant with broad, sweeping vistas of tall mountains and complex valleys. The land was for sale at a very reasonable price and the owners were anxious to sell. Everything was in place. Estée and I were very excited. We went back many times to sit on the large boulders that were scattered around the property and both of us got goose bumps considering the possibilities of outside verandas with bougainvillea, palms, and Australian bottle brush trees.

Finally, the day came when we would write the check to finalize the purchase. We were to meet the family who owned the land. We had the address in Gualaceo and the architect was to meet us there. He told us there were a few things about the land he needed to check on; just routine things. We knocked at the door of the house at the appointed time, which is very un-Ecuadorian. (Being on time in Ecuador is essentially unheard of; something we have confirmed many times since.) Checkbook in hand, we were shown into a nice, well-furnished house. We were offered, and accepted, a small glass of warm *cañalazo*, a rum drink with herb additives that was made right there on the property.

The architect showed up a half hour later. He did not smile. He looked at Estée and me with a tired and sympathetic expression. He knew we really wanted this piece of land and all the promise it provided. He had even once said that if we did not buy it, he would. He started to speak slowly, and his voice actually quivered for a few words. "I would advise you not to buy this land," was his shocking pronouncement. He continued, "I found out from the government planning office in Cuenca that there are plans to build a municipal sewage treatment plant on the lower two-thirds of the land you are about to purchase. Your home would overlook three huge sewage-holding tanks. There is no starting date to build these, but at some point, the city of Gualaceo could annex that portion of your land and build these sewage tanks."

We were too stunned to respond. We had our checkbook out, ready to sign. The family members sat silently, looking down at their feet. They had known this all along. Finally, one family member looked up and said cheerfully, "Aah, that will never happen, don't worry about it."

In October of 2005, we came back to Gualaceo for the First Andean Orchid Congress, a scientific examination of the distribution and pollination of the orchids of Ecuador, among other subjects. We thought this would give us another opportunity to view hilltops and swampland, and generally find a lot more places where we did not want to build our house. Estée had less interest in the scientific details of the orchid genus Pleurothallis than I did (and my interest was fairly limited), so she took the opportunity to look for the perfect plot of land. She found more hilltops for sale and some swampland in or near flood plains, but until the last day of the conference, there was nothing.

I was doggedly sitting through the last lecture on orchid DNA and had just asked what I thought was a brilliant question regarding the evolutionary forces that might lead to the incorporation of viral genes into orchid DNA when Estée burst into the back of the room, waving to me with an excited look on her face. I tried to ignore her since I thought my question was actually a good one.

She marched up to me and announced that I needed to come immediately. There was a cook at the local school who had heard that we were looking for some land. He had driven Estée earlier that afternoon to a place he knew was for sale. The land, in Estée's opinion, was ideal. It was only a short distance from the ideal piece of costly land on the San Francisco River we had seen before, the one with Fox News on cable TV. I spent about ten minutes walking around the property and immediately called the architect. He arrived shortly afterward and gave us his stamp of approval.

The land was mostly pasture and sloped gently down to the rapidly flowing and heavenly sounding river. There were some shrubs and trees by the river and around a ruin of a *casita* high up on the property. It was about three acres of land and access required a short bumpy ride on a steep, sloping road from the main dirt thoroughfare to Macas. The valley in which our prospective little piece of land sat ran exactly east to west, with mountains surrounding the valley on all sides. The breezes were predominantly from the east, carrying moist air from the Amazon basin up over the mountains 7,500 feet to where our home would be situated.

Now, all we had to do was to buy the land. We left for Chicago the next day, so we had no word about who owned it or the price they might ask. We got word a week later that the architect had used his wily ways to negotiate a fair price. We were now proud owners of foreign property. We were thrilled, if not a little overwhelmed. Could it get any better? Well, since you asked, yes, it could. We still really needed to sell our house in Oak Park (quit laughing). But we were happy and we felt near the top. Herein lies a problem. If you think you are near the top, there is really only one direction to go—down, down, and further down, into the hellhole of moving, and then construction!

chapter 3

The Move:
New Adventures in Night Sweats

As I laid on a gurney at West Suburban Hospital in east Oak Park on a Monday morning in 1995, the emergency room physician asked me questions about my symptoms. I had spent a restless night tossing and turning and generally keeping Estée awake with my fussing and fidgeting. The next morning, I got out of bed and passed out on the floor with what I was told later was a loud thump. With help, I made it downstairs to the couch, mainly so the 911 responding paramedics would not have to carry me down the narrow stairs and likely drop me.

During the question-and-answer session in the emergency room, I was asked if I'd had night sweats the night before. I had, in fact, soaked the sheets, but I attributed that to the nightmares I'd had after seeing the Chicago Bears get whipped yet again the day before. The physician's response was "if you sweat, we sweat," and I got carted off in another ambulance to Rush-Presbyterian St. Luke's, where I had previously worked. After several medical adventures, including the misdiagnosis that I was dying of annular carcinoma of the small intestine with metastases to the liver, my gall bladder was removed and I was fine. Actually, I was not really fine until the nasal-gastric tube was removed—then I was fine. Years later, when I began to arrange for the move to Ecuador, I completely redefined night sweats.

Moving across the street is not easy. Moving across town or across the country is less easy. Moving to Ecuador is something else entirely. The very first precious item we needed to move was our one-and-a-half-year-old Doberman named Pepper. He was a beautiful 105-pound red Doberman with a lap-dog personality. If we did not move anything else, we needed to move him. Estée said that if Pepper did not move to Ecuador, she did not move to Ecuador. She would wish me well in my future, should I have one. I believed her. In fact, I felt the same way. The plan was that Pepper and I would move to Ecuador where we would supervise the initial phases of construction on our new doghouse and human house, respectively. Estée would stay in Chicago and supervise the selling of our house in Oak Park (quit laughing) and get ready to move our stuff.

We went to the Ecuadorian Consulate on Michigan Avenue in Chicago to see exactly what had to be done to move a dog—not just any dog, but Pepper. We were told by well-meaning people that, yes, it was possible to move a dog to Ecuador, but why, in God's name, were we moving to Ecuador? After many questioning looks from the staff at the consulate, we were given a list of papers we had to assemble to accomplish the feat. I swear I heard someone mutter under his breath, "Are they loco?" The question was muttered in Spanish, but even then I knew the word "loco."

The challenge of moving Pepper was somewhat like a treasure hunt, the prize being to wake up in Ecuador with those bright amber eyes staring at you, bad doggy breath breathing on you, and a distinct sense of urgency to get outside for the morning pee.

The length of the list of items on the treasure hunt was not trivial, but most things made sense, including an overall health check-up for Pepper, an up-to-date rabies shot, a stamp of approval by the U.S. Department of Agriculture, and a document stipulating that the dog could be in temperatures ranging from a low of forty-five degrees Fahrenheit to a high of eighty-five degrees for more than forty-five minutes. This temperature restriction was a little tricky since we were trying to move Pepper from Chicago through Miami to Guayaquil, Ecuador, in the middle of January. The temperature ranges in those three locations could be from far below forty-five degrees to far above eighty-five degrees. On top of these requirements, American Airlines had its own rules and regulations, some but not all of which were spelled out on their website.

I spent days accumulating the necessary documents, each one of which had to be notarized and have an Apostille attached. An Apostille, I discovered, is an impressive-looking document with stamps and gold seals all over it that vouches that the notary public who notarized your document is actually a notary public and that the document is truly legal. It dates to a treaty signed in 1962 of which both the U.S. and Ecuador are signatories. Who would have guessed? Our veterinarian, Marla, helped us a great deal, and we got all the items together. Now it was time to deal with American Airlines.

There are many things in the world that are impossible, and getting in touch with an actual person on the phone at any airline to get some answers on how to ship a dog to Ecuador is very high on the impossible list. We were now in mid-November, and while Estée and I had our tickets, and Pepper had his reservation to travel, we needed to make certain we had all the information we needed. I found the only way to get that information was to go to O'Hare Airport to the American Airlines check-in counter. I learned the type and dimensions of the crate we should use, the temperature restrictions, the fact that we had to be at the airport three hours before departure, and that the dog would not be let out in Miami, so he would be in his crate until we met again in Guayaquil. American Airlines had lost a show dog, a Westminster champion show dog no less, in the airport in Miami a few months before, so the rules had been changed accordingly.

Everything seemed set to go, but as I was turning to leave, the representative asked, "How much does your dog weigh? You know there is a limit of one hundred pounds total. The dog and the crate must weigh less than one hundred pounds." I froze. I knew that the dog was about 105 pounds, but I did not know how much the crate weighed. It turned out to weigh thirty pounds. So here we were about a month and a half before flight time finding out that we were thirty-five pounds overweight.

The Tom Hanks movie *Apollo 13* is one of my favorites. I imagined all the astronauts and flight engineers tasked with finding how to reduce the combination of dog and crate by thirty-five pounds before liftoff. We could put the dog on a strict diet, we could try to find a lighter crate that was still approved by the airlines, or we could try to find another airline that did not have that restriction. The strict diet might buy us five pounds at most. This was a big dog, not a fat dog. We might find an approved crate that was five pounds lighter. Together, we might starve and shave off ten pounds, which would still leave us twenty-five pounds over. I called Delta and Continental, got someone by claiming an emergency both times, and discovered that neither airline carried pets internationally other than in freight. Even then there was no guarantee that your pet would fly with you or at all.

In desperation, Estée accompanied me back to O'Hare and back to the check-in counter at American. There we met a wonderful lady who listened to our story. Estée explained that we tried to put the dog on a diet, but we could not expect to starve thirty-five pounds off him. American Airlines approved no other crate. We were at wit's end. The check-in lady was quite a bit overweight herself, and both Estée and I sensed that we might have found a sympathetic ear in our attempts to force weight off the poor dog. She made a few calls, then a few more calls, and finally told us she would approve Pepper's travel document. There would be no extra charge for his "overweight" status. She gave us her full name and her personal phone number, and told us to call her if we had any problems during check-in. You see—you still can have good experiences at an airline check-in counter.

On January 10, 2007, we got to the airport with Pepper three hours early. We met our good friends, Carlos and Marti, who proved that friends will help you move and real friends will help you move a body—Pepper's, in this case. The international check-in area in concourse three at O'Hare was nearly empty at this hour, and while the personnel at the check-in counters played with Pepper, our papers were scrutinized to the last signature and the last Apostille by a hostile check-in person. She even called to check temperatures at all locations through which Pepper would be traveling. It seemed like this check-in person was hell-bent on seeing that we did not travel with Pepper that day. She was outwardly disappointed that she could not find a single reason to block his travel, so we petted him good-bye and off we went in our different directions— all toward the same plane.

Our connections were miraculously on time. Estée made certain that the flight attendants and the pilot on the plane from Miami to Guayaquil knew that there was a puppy onboard. The pilot went below to check and came back to Estée to ask if the huge Doberman was the puppy she was referring to. We were truly on our way.

"Welcome to Guayaquil," the sign said. Pepper, in his crate, came through the rubber baffles that prevent people from seeing their luggage being thrown unceremoniously onto the conveyer belt that carries what is left of their belongings to them. Pepper was looking out the little windows on the side of the crate, and I really wonder what was going through his mind. I am sure the "Welcome to Guayaquil" sign didn't mean much.

It was an incredible feeling of relief to see his nose pressed up against the crate window. Customs waived us to the head of the line, and without X-raying Pepper or our luggage, which is always done upon arrival in Ecuador, we were told to get out of the airport right away. I tried to hand them my inch-thick documentation with Apostilles containing the gold seals and all the stamps that would allow Pepper to enter Ecuador with the greatest of legality, but they would not even have it forced upon them. Their total concern was the sanctity of their relatively urine-free floors. Pepper peed for about five minutes outside on the airport trees and shrubbery, and then he peed some more. During the fourteen-hour trip, he did not have an "accident" in his crate; he was a well-trained, if stressed, dog.

I had corresponded with unknown people at the Sheraton Four Points in Guayaquil to be certain that we could keep Pepper with us. I had promised that he would be a good dog. During our trips back and forth from Chicago to Ecuador, we had stayed at the Sheraton several times. I talked to unknown people during these trips. I had shown them pictures of Pepper, admittedly as a much-smaller puppy, but still…I had emails from unknown personnel from the Sheraton stating unequivocally that Pepper would be very welcome. As I approached the very pleasant-looking young girl at the reservation desk, I saw a frown form on her face that drew her black eyebrows toward each other and created deep, unsightly wrinkles on her forehead. Before she had a chance to speak, I presented the reservation, the emails from various unknown persons (who *used to* work at the Sheraton, it turned out), and my very best pleading look. Then I asked for the manager.

The manager came around the corner and did not frown. He was too shocked. Pepper was quietly sitting beside Estée and me, minding his own business. The manager looked at the paperwork, and like the check-in person at O'Hare, he tried to find any excuse he could to reject our reservation for Pepper. He could not. We were in. At checkout, Pepper came down with us and sat patiently while the manager had someone check the room and then recheck it. We were proud of Pepper when the manager told us that he was the best dog he had ever seen. Pepper, he told us, could have a standing reservation at the Sheraton Four Points. I am sure that manager is gone by now.

After the successful night at the Sheraton, we were picked up in a van for the trip through the Cajas to Gualaceo, where Pepper's doghouse and our human house were to be built. There was not one bark, not one whine, not a whimper from Pepper from the time he entered Ecuador until the moment he saw his first llama at the pass in the Cajas at 14,000 feet. He teed off at that llama as if it was his worst enemy, even though he had never seen one before. It was as if he associated that llama with the whole experience, and it was his turn to express himself. I could not have agreed more.

On paper, it appeared that the most daunting task in our plans to retire to Ecuador would be to arrange and execute the physical move of our accumulated stuff. That turned out to be wrong. The most daunting task was to sell our house. We, of course, thought our house was worth a lot and would sell quickly. Our real estate agents also thought our house was worth a lot, but their "lot" was considerably less than our "lot," and they were not at all sure it would sell quickly. Upon announcing that our house was for sale, one friend inquired as to how much we were asking and thought it would sell in a week. Buoyed by this optimism, we sat by the phone to wait for the highest bidder, thinking that the bid might even be over the asking price. After all, a year or two before, houses in our area were selling by word of mouth and fetching very high prices.

The phone did not ring. Unbeknownst to us, the housing market had crossed the horizon of a giant black hole and was in free fall. Our real estate agents tried to be kind and gentle, tried to encourage, tried to explain the avarice and mistakes in the banking industry. They tried very hard to sell our house. They had many open houses with colorful balloons attached to brightly painted signs and, at first, people came. They were mostly people in the area who were planning to put their houses on the market and wanted to see the competition. After a few months, fewer people came. At the time our house was on the market, there were over forty other houses for sale in a fifteen-square-block area in North Oak Park. It seemed like all of North Oak Park was for sale and no one was buying.

After many months went by, we lowered the price. This did no good. It was clear that something in the housing market had gone terribly wrong. *Bloomberg Financial News*, along with thirty other financial TV stations and publications, bore this out. By now, we had purchased the land in Ecuador, approved the housing plans, and were ready to move, so that is what we decided to do: move.

Over eons, humans have developed a relationship to their possessions that goes far beyond utility. At some point in time, one caveman bragged to his neighbor who lived in the cave north of him, "My club is bigger than yours." "Oh, yeah?" came the reply. "Well, my club is made out of finer wood than yours." (Yes, the cavemen spoke English; I am sure of it.) At that point in history, the possession race was on.

John, a friend from Australia, defended his purchases of things non-utilitarian to his wife by confidently stating, "He who dies with the most toys, wins." Exactly what "he" wins is unclear. When faced with a move of any kind, you cannot help but reflect on the relationship between you and your possessions. Do your possessions define you? Do you present yourself to the world through the stuff you own? We thought about and discussed these questions as we wrestled with the list of what to bring to Ecuador.

There was a category of stuff that was clearly utilitarian and high on the list of things to take with us, like clothes, shoes, dishes, silverware, towels, and dog bowls. In this case, it was a question of how many or how much to pack. There were things toward the middle of the spectrum that would be nice to have, like a leaf blower or a hedge trimmer. If we really needed these, we could get them in Ecuador (well, the leaf blower might be a stretch). Then there were many things that were borderline, such as the eight books on how to paint seascapes—something I thought I really wanted to do in retirement. (As silly as it may seem, I still want to do that even though we ended up nowhere near the sea.)

Then there was the other end of the spectrum: things that I could not even give away, like my size 52 nurse's dress, the double-D bra that I stuffed with ten white tube socks, five to a side, and my blond wig—all part of a Halloween costume that I thought would be even less dignified if worn in Ecuador. All the Halloween costumes, including my French maid ensemble and my sparkling fairy godmother wings and magic wand, went into the trash. At this point, I did not care what the garbage men or the scavengers thought.

It turned out that it was not just a utilitarian judgment that we made when we decided to include or exclude an item from the shipping containers. The attached memories came into play. Most of our stuff was not particularly valuable, but it had memories attached. In the end, those things and their memories provided a valuable continuity that helped us bridge the two locations and the two continents. So now, it was time to make the decisions: What stuff and memories would we include on our English, translated into Spanish, shipping list?

Estée and I had lived in one house for over twenty-five years, so we had a lot of stuff. That stuff was in the garage, in the basement, in the attic, and, in the case of the stuff that we actually used, scattered unevenly around our three-story English Tudor–style home. We had given a lot of hours of thought to what we needed to bring and what we wanted to bring. We had, by then, the plans for the new house we were building in Ecuador, and we also had an idea of the construction and household items that were either scarce, non-existent, or over twice the price at stores near where we were going to live. We needed to bring much of our furniture, all of our appliances, all our lighting, and all the door handles. When this stuff was added to the garden supplies, the Christmas trees and ornaments from our great neighbors, Bill and Bob, and the purchases from Costco, which included an outdoor patio heater, large mirrors, an ice maker, and much more, it was clear that two forty-foot containers were required.

As soon as our house in Oak Park had gone on the market (quit laughing), we'd been inundated with mail and phone calls from movers. I was impressed with how attuned the moving industry was to the buying and the attempted selling of houses and the comings and goings of people and their stuff. We decided to get three bids, which I was told was the proper method of selecting a mover. The bids were wildly different. One company was nearly twice the price of the other two. While we had some artwork that we liked, none of it was painted or even sketched by Rembrandt, Cézanne, or Picasso. It was painted or sketched by Frank, Joe, and Debby. The high-bidding company felt it necessary to build an elaborate wood crate for each piece of art, which would cost thousands of dollars. While we appreciated their assessment of our art almost as much as we appreciated the art itself, I doubt that an insurance company would have agreed with their assessment.

The low bid came from a phone call. The very nice woman on the other end of the line responded to my inquiry as to when the company could send someone to give an estimate by saying, "We don't need to see it; I can give you the estimate right now on the phone." We chose the middle estimate.

After our due diligence, we settled on McCollister's to be our mover. Their representative, Mr. Jensen, came to the house and instilled confidence by assuring me that McCollister's moved people all over the world. He listed all the countries that McCollister's had moved people to and from. The list did not include Ecuador. He mentioned that moving people to Ecuador could not be more difficult than moving people to Iraq, which was on his list. What could go wrong? I thought the same thing. What, indeed, could go wrong?

It turned out that a lot could go wrong. The move was to take place in September of 2007. I had been living in Ecuador in a rental house since January of that year, and I came back to Chicago to help pack. What I really did, pretty much, was stand around and watch. The packers did a good job, judging by the fact that when we unpacked, most of our stuff was unbroken. How else can you tell?

One of the rules of Ecuador at the time was that you had to have the containers and all your stuff inspected. Evidently, this was to ensure that you were not bringing in cases of cigarettes or stinger missiles. Ecuador had an arrangement with an "inspection" company headquartered in Miami. I called to see what the rules were and how we were to go about arranging the inspection. I got very little information but was essentially told to go ahead and pack our stuff and put it in the containers. That is what we did. This turned out to be a costly mistake.

The filled containers pulled away and Estée and I walked around the empty house. The sounds of our footsteps and the timbre of our voices reverberated from the empty walls and floors producing an eerie and sobering feeling. The sight of the containers moving around the corner and out of sight marked the end of a phase of our lives that had lasted a long time. The house had a lot of happy memories associated with it. The unhappy memories were thankfully few and had been forgotten, as humans have the great capacity to do.

Some of the happiest memories were of the New Year's Eve parties we hosted annually for almost twenty years. It started out as a neighborhood party, a small local event so that everyone could enjoy him or herself and crawl home rather than risk life and limb on the roads after midnight. After a few years, the party expanded with the inclusion of friends outside the area as well. The party peaked in 1994 when we had about sixty people, seemingly half of whom were Puerto Rican. It all started with a practical joke.

We knew that our Puerto Rican friend, Carlos, and his Irish wife, Marti, were coming in a limousine and staying the night. We also knew the name of the limousine company. About a week before the party, Estée called Carlos and disguised her Hungarian-accented voice to the point that Carlos did not know who was on the other end. Estée asked Carlos to confirm the limousine reservation.

"Sir, I am calling to confirm that you made a reservation for one limousine to take two people from your residence in Bartlett, Illinois, to North Oak Park. Is that correct?"

Carlos replied, "Yes, that is correct."

"You will be leaving Bartlett at six o'clock?"

Carlos replied, "Yes."

"You will be paying cash, is that correct?"

"Yes, that's right," said Carlos.

"Sir, there is just one more thing that might present a problem. I'm sorry that I have to ask, but I understand that your last name is Sanchez, is that correct?"

His answer came a little slow and with some degree of apprehension in his voice. "Yes, my last name is Sanchez."

"Sir, is that a Puerto Rican name?" asked Estée in a well-disguised voice. The answer came with more than a hint of anger beginning to surge through the phone connection. "Yes, I am Puerto Rican," came Carlos's loud and partly combative answer.

Estée said, barely able to contain her laughter, "Well, sir, I must inform you that this limousine company is not allowed to take Puerto Ricans to Oak Park. Oak Park is a nice community, you know."

There was dead silence. Finally, Carlos broke the tension.

"Estée, is that you?"

"Yes."

There was a string of expletives both in English and in Puerto Rican–style Spanish, followed by reluctant laughter and the comment, "Okay, you got me."

Two days later, Carlos called Estée to ask if it was okay if his mom and dad came to the party. "Yes, of course," Estée said. The next night, Carlos called again to ask if his brother and his brother's wife and daughter could come. "Of course," Estée said with a smile. The third night, Carlos called again. His aunt and uncle were coming to town, and would it be okay if they came as well? Estée gleefully said, "Yes, of course it is fine. If you have any other Puerto Rican friends, invite them all as well." Estée thought this was all a joke, payback for her limousine prank.

On New Year's Eve, Estée opened the door to find Carlos and nineteen Puerto Rican relatives at the door. By the end of the evening, we had to borrow wine from our neighbors. It was the best party we ever hosted.

This and many other memories flooded through our minds as we sat on the two chairs that were not going to Ecuador. In the evening, it was particularly eerie. The sound of footsteps on the bare tiger-oak floors echoed around the empty rooms as we walked around the empty house, reminiscing. We knew we would miss our friends and our routine: our lives as we had lived them for so many years. Yet a sense of adventure and curiosity drove us forward. We were committed, and if it didn't work out, we were truly screwed.

Meanwhile, the two containers holding all of our stuff were driven off to a warehouse. McCollister's, the moving company, was baffled by the inspection. No other country, including Iraq, required such an inspection. We gave them the information of the Ecuador-approved inspection company in Miami, but that did little good. It took thirty days for the inspection to finally take place. The surly manager at the inspection company told us that we should not have loaded up all our stuff in the containers. All the stuff should have been inspected before it was loaded up. This did not make any sense to me, since we could have added cases of cigarettes and stinger missiles after the inspection. Oh well. There really was no recourse. The inspection was completed after the thirty days. The moving company had to remove every item, unpack it, and repack it in front of the inspectors. I have never spent $9,500 in a more unpleasant way; and remember, this was in addition to the total cost of the move.

Finally, word came that our containers were on their way to New Jersey. There, the Chinese containers would be loaded onto a Chinese container ship and transported to the Panama Canal. Notice, I said *to* the Panama Canal, not *through* the Panama Canal. It is no wonder that there are more new billionaires in China than in any other country. I think many of those new billionaires are in the shipping industry. The cost of actually taking a container vessel through the Panama Canal is so high that a whole new industry has sprung up around it. Now, many Chinese container ships coming from the east in the Gulf of Mexico have their containers unloaded by Chinese workers in Colon, Panama, where the containers are loaded onto railroad cars and transported to the other side of Panama near Panama City. Chinese workers reload the containers onto Chinese ships and they resume their journey.

Our containers were off-loaded on the Atlantic side of Panama and transported to the Pacific side. There, the journey came to a screeching halt. There was a strike by workers who were responsible for loading the containers onto the ships. Our containers sat in the Panama sun, day after day, for nearly two months. We knew this because we called the moving company almost every day, first in a panic, then with the increasingly sinking feeling that we may never see our stuff again, and if we did, it may be baked to the point of over-done.

In late December of 2007, we were informed that the strike was over and that one of our containers was on the way. Was that okay? I thought it was fine, but wow, was I wrong. The broker in the port of entry in Ecuador hit the roof. Actually, he was outside, but if he were inside, he would have hit the roof. It turns out that the paperwork was made out for two containers, and if only one came, it would still be accepted. However, when the second container arrived, there would be no corresponding paperwork, and it would be sent back to its point of origin. For us, it would be a crapshoot as to which half of our stuff we would get. We were very happy that the broker caught this. The container on the ship had to be taken back to Panama and paired up physically with the second one. On December 27, we got the call that both containers had arrived in Guayaquil, Ecuador.

The containers had to be inspected again in Guayaquil, but this was fairly perfunctory. Satisfied that we had not added cigarettes or stinger missiles to the inventory, the Ecuadorian moving company trucked the forty-foot-high containers through the Cajas, past Pepper's arch-enemy the llama, past Cuenca, then on to Gualaceo on the Pan American Highway. The "high" part of the forty-foot-high container adds two feet to the height of the container compared to the normal height. This added two feet was just enough to take out most, but not quite all, of the electric wires and cables that crisscrossed the main street in Gualaceo. Many alarm clocks froze in time at 6:38 a.m. as the first of the tandem of container trucks made its way slowly through Gualaceo. Anyone watching would have seen a spectacular light show of sparks showering down from the broken lines. I am glad I was not there. I would have broken into a sweat yet again.

Now we had our stuff. What we did not have yet was a place to put it. It was time to build our house. This was going to take some time and during this time, we wanted to drive around our new environment and explore just where we were going to live. To do this, we needed a car.

chapter 4

Driving in Ecuador:
Forty-Seven Ways to Lose Your Life Before 7 p.m.

The human body is an incredible machine. We, as partly educated, semi-intelligent humans, firmly believe that we are the culmination of millions of years of evolution. (Oh, there is a contrary view that we, and everything around us, were all created on Sunday, October 23, 4004 B.C., but when this idea was put forward in 1650 by archbishop James Ussher, the other bishops, the archbishops, the cardinals, even the pope had a bit of a chuckle over that one. Nuns were not allowed to chuckle at that time.) Any outsider who has driven a rental car in Ecuador on vacation (brave soul) or as a retired expatriate (even braver) knows that it would take millions of years to evolve the skills to survive at the wheel in Quito, Cuenca, or especially Guayaquil, let alone in the rural areas of Ecuador. One's ability to survive depends largely on controlled vehicular agility in a traffic mix where one out of a thousand drivers has even heard of drivers' education. Okay, I exaggerate. It is much more like one out of ten thousand.

Transportation is critical for humankind. Ever since the wheel was invented, we humans have been hell-bent on producing bigger, faster, and deadlier road transportation. We invented large to huge trucks, big to gigantic buses, mini to tall top-heavy vans, with the trend now toward very small to slightly larger, highly squashable cars. In Ecuador, the mix of all these vehicles produces a swirling mass of engine noise, black smoke, foul smells, steel and plastic, dark diesel clouds, swirling colors, colorless and odorless CO_2, and constant and insistent honking. Oh, the honking! The honking is especially irritating because it is designed to exhort one to enter the swirling mass and join the free-for-all. Estée and I were very anxious to join the hurly-burly known as "driving" in Ecuador.

Our house was going to be located about two kilometers outside of Gualaceo, and we clearly needed transportation. We wanted something that could go to the jungle, so an SUV seemed to be the vehicle of choice. In Chicago, we both drove cars every day. We drove on the Eisenhower Expressway, Lake Shore Drive, the Kennedy Expressway, and many other traffic-packed, accident-laden highways and streets in and around the city. Neither of us had been in a serious accident, so we felt that if we could drive in Chicago, we could drive anywhere. We had no idea how wrong we were.

When Estée and I showed up in Ecuador to actually begin retirement, one of our first priorities was to get a car. Carlos and Marti, who accompanied us, were going to stay for only ten days. We wanted to see some Ecuadorian sights. Besides, Estée was going back to Chicago with them to try to sell our house (quit laughing), so I would be alone in about ten days. I really, really, needed transportation.

Carlos is much more knowledgeable about the ins and outs of car buying than I am. I generally kick the tires, gaze at the engine, and pretend to have a clue, while at the same time praying that no one asks me anything about tires or engines. I was grateful when Carlos, along with our Ecuadorian friend Pepe, decided to accompany me to Cuenca to buy a car. I told our Ecuadorian friends the plan and they patted me on the back and said some reassuring words like "sure, good luck with that" and "see you when you get back with your new car." They also muttered some less-than-reassuring words under their breath like "no way." They said these things in sarcastic Spanish. I did not speak even regular Spanish, so I smiled and thanked them for their best wishes, not having any idea what they were really saying or the failure they were predicting.

The cars I looked at in the U.S. that I thought would get us to the jungle and most of the way back home were the Nissan and Toyota SUVs. They were available in Ecuador, so we stopped at the Nissan dealer first. We were informed that the one Pathfinder on the lot was $60,000 but another one could be brought from Quito. It was slightly more expensive at $68,000. More Spanish was spoken, and I assumed that the extra $8,000 was for some tires and at least part of an engine. Both Pepe and Carlos noted my smirk as I asked the dealer what the price was for Ecuadorians, as I was about to become one. I proudly displayed my passport containing my permanent resident visa stamp for the dealer's inspection. The dealer smirked back, which showed me that no dealing, no haggling, and no bargains were to be found. We marched on to the Toyota dealer, where the financial news was worse. I was beginning to sense that buying a car in Ecuador was not going to rate well in the section on "Economic Reasons to Move to Ecuador" in books in the travel/retirement section of Amazon.com.

In a short time, we found ourselves at the Ford dealer. I marched around the parking lot where the new cars were on display, kicking the tires, looking at the engines, and avoiding the salespersons. I settled on a Ford Explorer. The dealer, who knew Pepe, actually came down a bit on the price, and we had a deal at $45,000. The dealer explained that the cost of the car in Ecuador was $55,000 if the car was assembled in the U.S. This vehicle was assembled in Venezuela, which meant that it cost almost $10,000 less, owing mostly to labor costs. We had transferred funds down to our bank in Gualaceo for the purchase, and Pepe negotiated the finishing touches so we could drive the car home that day. The total experience took just over five hours, and we were on our way with Pepe at the wheel. I was not about to navigate the roads until I had some experience in the safer (I thought) hinterlands around Gualaceo.

Our friends were astonished to see us drive up with our brand-new green and tan Explorer. Those same friends also told us that they hoped we liked it because we would never be able to resell it. Ecuadorians only bought, in descending order, white, black, silver, and occasionally red cars. Didn't we know that? There is nothing like a little pinprick to let the air out of the euphoric atmosphere and the idea that we were moving forward in our Ecuador experience! At least now we had transportation.

Like me, one of Carlos's passions in life is photography. We have convinced each other that we are really good at it, although in our hearts we both know better. Still, we have fun, and occasionally we produce, quite by accident, something to which other people kindly say, "Wow, that is really…interesting." In our quest to produce another "wow" picture, we decided one evening over a glass of wine that we would head southwest to a place where the wily red poison dart frog was known to reside. We thought that the wily red poison dart frog would be a worthy "wow" subject for our near-professional (in our minds) skill. At the last minute, we procured, with the help of Pepe, a guide who knew where the frogs were hiding.

This was to be a day trip, so we got started at about 8:30 in the morning laden with ham sandwiches, coffee, plenty of water, a short ton of photographic equipment, rain gear, sun gear, mud gear, a map, GPS, and of course, the guide, along with Carlos and Marti. Estée, the brains of the family, stayed safely at home with Pepper, with the excuse that "someone has to stay with the dog; he is new to Ecuador and he's lonely." Off we went. I was the driver, Ivan the guide was beside me, and Carlos and Marti were in the back seat. All safety belts were securely fastened and though I thought I could hear the very faint hint of muttered prayers, I assured myself that those were just new-car noises.

All went smoothly through Cuenca and toward Loja, where we came upon a detour because of road construction. The detour took us on a dirt road through beautiful pastoral country surrounded by mountains on all sides. Adobe houses dotted the countryside as the morning sun lit up the valley. A smile came across my face and I thought, "Ah, this is why we retired to Ecuador." Children of all ages in their colorful school uniforms were walking on each side of the road, going the same way we were, on their way to school. I was carefully picking my way through the gauntlet of kids when I glanced in my rearview mirror. I fully expected to see the heads of Carlos and Marti, the dirt road behind us, and the faces of the colorfully dressed kids we were passing. What I saw was grillwork with the three-pointed star of the Mercedes logo. I could see bits of butterflies and moths on the logo and the surrounding grillwork. I did not dare to look very long without wiping out a row of school kids (even though I was driving at a speed consistent with conditions, as I had been taught to do in drivers' education).

Then the horn sounded. It startled everyone in the car, including me. It was not just loud; it had an unearthly sound that provided a true warning of impending doom if prompt action were not taken on my part. It was quite clear that the prompt action was to get the hell out of the way. Given the gauntlet of kids, the lack of adjoining roads, and the one-lane status of the road we were on, we were trapped. I tried to accelerate, but that was dangerous because of the kids, and even though I managed a few miles an hour faster, the grillwork seemed closer. Now I could see bits of flies and mosquitoes. I tried honking back, but that seemed to infuriate whoever or whatever it was that was hell-bent on our destruction. The movie *The Duel* with Dennis Weaver crossed my mind. I looked for a cliff. The tension in the Explorer was palpable.

After what seemed like an hour but was probably only a minute or two of constant harassment, I found an opportunity. We were past the kids now, and there was an adjoining road where I could pull off to the right. I did so with a maneuver that would have made race car driver Jimmy Johnson proud. With a blaring blast of the horn, a gray-blue blur went careening by, followed inches behind by a horn-blaring red blur. We sat silently for several minutes as the two city buses full of people, each driven by a young insane Latino male, raced each other to their destination at break-neck speeds. I thought of the horror stories of buses falling off cliffs in the Andes, killing dozens of people, and began to understand how some of those accidents might happen.

This was my first encounter with Latino machismo, and it was a valu-able lesson, one that is not taught in drivers' education. Conversation slowly returned to the interior of the Explorer, all centered on "what the hell was that all about?" Our guide, Ivan, entertained us for much of the rest of the road trip with stories starting with, "You haven't seen anything yet. Let me tell you about the time…"

We made it to the frog habitat and discovered that it had nearly been destroyed by road construction. There was a small section remaining. We waded into a swampy, cow-dung muddied, smelly, up-to-your-ankles, just-over-your-boots water hole. We never saw a frog of any kind, let alone the wily red poison dart frog. I snapped a shot of Carlos looking forlorn as he was listening to the little chirps of what Ivan assured us was, indeed, the wily red poison dart frog. Whenever we got to within fifty feet of the sound, the chirping stopped. I knew that part of that chirp was actually a frog version of a laugh.

We drove home through an hour of dense fog, which seemed easy after our earlier encounter with the racing buses. We did not rush out of the car and kiss the ground when we got back into the driveway, but we were happy to be home. I had survived my first real driving experience in Ecuador.

Carlos and Marti, along with Estée, left from the Cuenca Airport on a Tuesday morning flight on AroGal to Guayaquil. Wednesday, they flew

American to the hell-port called Miami International. After flight delays and damaged luggage reports in Miami, they were off to Chicago.

I was home alone. I drove back from dropping them off at the airport in Cuenca and opened the front door of the rental house I was to occupy for a full year and a half while our house was being built. I opened the door to find the excited and expectant eyes of our Doberman, Pepper. Our eyes met, and while we had a special relationship, he quickly looked around my leg for Estée and the guarantee she provided that he would be fed in a timely fashion. I have rarely seen a look of true panic on a dog's face other than when faced with overwhelming and life-threatening odds on the battlefield of the Oak Park dog park on a Sunday morning. Even then, Dobermans rarely have a look of panic. They generally evoke that look in others. This was a look of true panic.

As the days and weeks unfolded, Pepper discovered that I usually remembered my daily chores as they related to him. The owners of the rental house had put a secure fence around the yard, and Pepper had a play yard the size of our whole lot in Oak Park. Pepper had dog toys, including balls and furry animal-like things, that he would toss into the air at least twice before the eyes and the cotton stuffing were ripped savagely from without and from within. The neighborhood dogs would line the outside of the fence in wonder and amazement.

For his part, Pepper would have loved to turn the area inside the fence into an Oak Park–style dog park. One small suicidal dog found a small hole in the fence and made his way into Pepper's play area. I had to put leather gloves on to rescue a screaming, terrified little dog as Pepper tried to play with him. I think the little dog saw the stuffing of the toy animals lying about the play area and thought his stuffing would join the cotton stuffing shortly.

Life settled into a routine. I was anxious to break up the monotony, so I was happy when I received a call from Ingrid, Pepe's wife, on a Thursday to ask if I wanted to accompany her and a friend the next day to a meeting in Lemon, a small town east of Gualaceo. I asked if I could drive since I needed the practice. The nightmares of my encounter with the bus race on the way to photograph the wily red poison dart frog had begun to subside. I arranged for someone to let Pepper out during the day and picked up the two women at eight in the morning.

Within ten feet of leaving the Gualaceo city limits, the road became an unfinished mess of unconnected potholes of varying depths, interspersed with rocks ranging from pebbles to boulders. Unfinished is a kind word. Gut-wrenching, bone-jarring, tire-shredding, axel-breaking, shock-absorber-flattening, car-destroying, rock-infested path is less kind but much more accurate. To get around Ecuador, you have to know how to survive these kinds of roads.

We bounced east and slightly north of Gualaceo for four and a half hours before arriving, exhausted, for the meeting. The meeting, which I thought was taking place, really was not taking place. The principle person, whom we were to meet, was not there. No one seemed to know where he was. Those in attendance were very friendly, but they were not empowered to make any decisions, so it was a non-meeting meeting. However, everyone kissed multiple times anyway, which I find endearing. If this were to happen in the United States, there certainly would be animosity toward the people who did not show up, especially after a four-and-a-half-hour ride on gut-wrenching roads. There would be no kissing.

After an hour of non-meeting but much kissing, we started home. It was 2:15 in the afternoon, and I was happy to get started since I did not want to have my second driving experience in Ecuador to be in the dark with racing buses.

Things went quite smoothly for the first two hours. We settled into a bouncing, bone-jarring rhythm and enjoyed the breathtaking scenery that was on every side of us in the Andes of southern Ecuador. Once again, that smile crossed my lips as I recounted the list of pros and cons Estée and I had put together that put the finishing touches on our decision to move to Gualaceo.

My smile, as I contemplated the long list of pros, came to an abrupt frown as I came to a halt behind two buses on a corner of the path called a road. The road curved to the right. At the bend, there was a mountain stream that came from the left. It was supposed to go into a tube built under the road and then continue down the thousand-foot drop-off on the immediate right of the road. The presence of road repair equipment, including a back-loader and men with shovels, suggested that the stream had found a different and, perhaps, more convenient path for itself, but with less convenient consequences for those of us who used the road to get from Lemon to Gualaceo. The first bus was a relatively small local bus and it was stuck in the mud on the corner. We were evidently fresh on the scene, since there were, at that point, few people, little discussion, and a small amount of hand waving. There were no vehicles facing us from the other side of the corner.

The second bus was a very large tourist bus that gave me terrible flashbacks and a slightly jerky tic because it had that Mercedes logo prominently displayed on the back. I could feel the cold sweats coming back. I was just happy to be stopped at the back of it rather than chased by the front of it. It was over half-full of German tourists, who were getting out of their bus to stretch and discuss and offer advice to the Spanish road workers in German. I quickly warmed to the potential entertainment value of the situation.

In a short time, vehicles of all descriptions began to accumulate on each side of the stuck-in-the-mud city bus. Now there was much discussion and a whole lot of hand waving. I think there was even the suggestion of tossing the bus over the thousand-foot cliff, but, evidently, that was vetoed, or else my Spanish was worse than I thought. Fortunately, the first vehicle to arrive on the other side of the corner was a large Hino truck. The driver had a heavy-duty chain and a means to attach it to the front of his vehicle. The back-loader filled in part of the corner with less-muddy soil containing some rock and, with little effort, the truck pulled the first bus safely to dry road. The German tourists got back into their bus. The accumulated crowd all rushed back to their vehicles of all different descriptions to try to pull out and get ahead of anything and every-thing ahead of them, and it appeared that the relatively short crisis was over.

BUT NO! For some reason known only to him, the driver of the German tour bus took the exact same bad angle through the corner that the city bus had taken. Not only did it get stuck, but as the driver attempted to accelerate, the wheels spun and the back of the bus started sliding on the black slippery mud slurry toward that thousand-foot drop off. I have been to many athletic events where human speed was a prime asset and greatly admired. Those ath-letes would have stood in awe as the well-fed, rotund, German tourists with snacks and cameras and hats in hand came roaring out of the front door of the tipped bus.

Since the line of vehicles of all descriptions did not move, people reluc-tantly turned off their engines, got out of their vehicles, and wandered toward the muddy corner once again. They quickly realized that now there was a real crisis. This was a seriously big bus on a seriously small road with the right front tire on one side of the corner and the rear right tires mired in mud on the other side of the corner. Under the bus, between the right front tire and the right rear tires was, well, space. This space was filled by the vision of distant jungle, and the distance was measured straight down in many, many feet. You could not simply pull this behemoth out of the muck and mire. This was going to take some engineering.

After much time that included discussions, shouting, hand waving, and head shaking, the operator of the back-loader hooked what looked to me to be a very thin chain to the back of the bus. A heavier chain was hooked onto the same Hino truck that pulled the smaller city bus out of peril. The bus driver did not look happy as he reentered the bus to drive it out (if the operation were a success) or to perhaps die (in an unsuccessful attempt). As the back-loader mangled and manhandled the back of the bus away from the ravine and the big Hino truck pulled the front forward, the bus driver slowly eased the bus onto dry and safe road. It was out.

As the tourists reentered the bus, very likely contemplating what their future held, the driver got out to survey the badly dented rear end of his precious vehicle. To my amusement, the Mercedes logo was mangled and hanging half off the back of the bus. I knew that this image would put a halt to my nightmares of the bus race. I could imagine the story the driver would concoct to tell the bus owners what had transpired. I'm sure it would involve other bus drivers with Latino machismo. I returned to the Explorer and it was my turn to go through the by-now infamous corner. Instead of rushing back to their vehicles this time, the accumulated crowd of nearly two hundred people gathered to watch the gringo go down the mountain.

I told Ingrid and her friend that they could walk across to the other side, but they feigned bravery and stayed in the car. I put the transmission into all-wheel drive and slowly drove at a proper angle to the other side. I clearly saw the look of disappointment in the spectators' eyes as I pulled onto dry, safe road. It was after 7 p.m. now and dark, just what I wanted to avoid. However, the rest of the trip was uneventful, and now I had my second major driving experience in Ecuador.

While cross-country driving presents challenges, local driving can as well. Gualaceo is an old town, and by old, I mean pre-Inca and older than Cuenca. It has a population of about 16,000 people with another 24,000 in the surrounding farms and villages. It is a town based almost solely on agriculture. At any moment in time, cows with or without ropes, cars of all description—including Datsun pickup trucks—burros, indigenous women weaving Panama hats, chickens, buses, people with huge bundles of assorted grasses for cuyes (guinea pigs), sheep, trucks of all sizes, dogs, defiant teenagers, bicycle-driven carts carrying purchases from the market or serving alcoholic beverages, uniformed school students, motorcycles, more dogs, unattended two-year-old children, goats, and slightly to grossly inebriated men can be seen converging on a single street corner. I am not making this up.

Two years ago, after years of discussion by the city council, a traffic light was erected at this corner. The light did not function, but its mere presence brought Gualaceo into the first half of the twentieth century—at least regarding traffic lights. One year ago, the light suddenly worked. This has created real havoc. No one knows what to do. After all, stop signs, and indeed all traffic-related signs, are often viewed as suggestions, not rules. A red light seems more of a rule-like thing, so confusion reigns. The indigenous Indians are perhaps the most confused because they are less likely to have been to major cities where one could be killed for crossing the street on a wrong-colored light. The solution of the city council to allay all this confusion has been to install more traffic lights to ease Gualaceo further into the twentieth century; however, this has multiplied the confusion. The indigenous Indians frequently wait in a sprinter-like stance at the intersection until the light turns green for cross-traffic, then commence in a true scurry directly into accelerating traffic as they dart toward the red light. It's never really a walk or a run, nor is it a sashay, a mince, or a glide; it really can only be described as a scurry, and a potentially deadly one at that. I have seen many near misses, but amazingly, I have never seen anyone hit. It is only a matter of time.

Gualaceo now boasts many sets of traffic lights at busy intersections and one set placed at each end of the one-lane, covered bridge that spans the Santa Barbara River. The set of lights at the bridge presents the biggest confusion. Prior to the lights, it was first come, first to enter, last to back down. After the lights were installed, the original rules still applied for some, while others waited patiently for a green light to proceed. They often found a car quickly entering from the other side and racing toward the other end of the plank-floored bridge at break-neck speed. Nearly four years have gone by after the installation of the lights and there has been only slight improvement.

There are large numbers of dangerous situations with which one is presented while driving in Ecuador. One is the left turn. Half the population believes that, with no exceptions, a blinking signal light on the driver's side of a car, bus, or truck means that the driver approaching from the rear should pull out and pass at maximum speed. The other half of the population believes that a blinking signal light on the driver's side of a vehicle means that the vehicle is actually going to turn left. This, of course, does not mean for a second that the approaching vehicle will not jam on the accelerator and try to pass before the left turn is accomplished. It just means that the driver of that vehicle thinks he can make it. This makes turning left a real adventure.

I mentioned the potential problem to some Ecuadorian friends, who confirmed my observations and said that the proper way to signal was to put your left hand straight out and signal the old-fashioned way. I nearly lost my hand and part of my lower arm. I have discovered that the best approach is to not signal at all. Now I turn on all the lights, flashing and non-flashing, flail my arms in all directions, honk the horn with intermittent short and long blasts, and make an abrupt lurch to the left. As silly as these things must look, they seem to produce mass amazement and allow enough time to make the left-turn maneuver. Having done this enough, I probably have the reputation of being a crazy gringo to watch out for, especially on those left turns.

Another dangerous situation is the "sleeping policeman" or the infamous speed bump. These are wildly popular throughout Ecuador. Some are sanctioned, and most of the sanctioned ones are marked, but not all. The unmarked ones are, quite literally, deadly ones. Several motorcyclists lose their lives each year by launching themselves into an inadvertent Evel Knievel aerial stunt without an end plan.

While speed bumps on major roads are well-marked and deadly if not heeded, the worst are the homemade ones on the country roads. These are almost never marked and blend into the overall road vision of potholes, pebbles, and boulders. I have nearly broken my own neck, not to mention the necks of my passengers, as I become completely airborne after hitting an unmarked speed bump at forty-five miles per hour. People living on the side of the road erect these unmarked country road speed bumps to slow traffic near their home to protect their children, chickens, cows, horses, and any other living thing that they hold dear. In some ways, I do not blame them, especially if I happen to see the speed bump and can slow down as they intended I should. My bone to pick is that some of these speed bumps are monuments to the building capabilities of humanity. They are mega structures, built more to be admired than to be driven over. They are designed to not only slow a vehicle down, but to send it cartwheeling down the road. I am sure that the whole family sits on the front porch near the speed bump, with lunch and drinks in hand, in great anticipation of their daily entertainment.

All of the obstacles I have described are formidable when the dogs, cows, chickens, horses, goats, sheep, more dogs, and humans are sober. Now mix in a little to a lot of alcohol, which seems to be confined to human consumption, and see what happens. *Zhumir* is a local alcoholic drink made from sugar cane. I assume it is a rum-like drink, but I have not tasted it. I value the thin layer of enamel still left on my teeth. *Zhumir* sells for a few dollars a liter and is sold in thick glass bottles, since it is reputed to eat through regular glass. *Zhumir* is just one of many alcoholic beverages that contribute to a growing problem of alcoholism in Ecuador. I do not judge people and what they drink, but I really don't want to hit a person after they have been imbibing excessively.

Ecuadorians pretty much live from fiesta to fiesta. Wouldn't it be great if the whole world were like that? Wouldn't it be great if the Jews and the Palestinians could just party down? Perhaps I am getting carried away.

Here, fiestas seem to occur weekly, but maybe it just seems so. Drinking large quantities of alcohol is a big part of each fiesta, so it is not unusual to see over-served people, particularly toward the end of the day. What's dangerous is that the over-served continue to serve themselves until they are completely overcome. They then lay down, pretty much wherever and in whatever peculiarly odd position, once they are unable to feel or find their mouth. This accounts for pairs of legs protruding from the sides of roads and sticking out into traffic, legs which can be easily run over if extreme caution is not exercised by drivers.

Recently, our Ecuadorian friends Joe and Lourdes were leaving our house. The electronic gate opened, and as Joe was driving out into the dark with his headlights on, he slammed on the brakes and got out of the car. We thought he had forgotten something, but we discovered that there was an over-served human lump in the middle of our drive just outside the gate. The over-served lump was dressed all in black, laying on a black drive on a black night. There were absolutely no safety reflectors to be found on the lump. It was very fortunate that Joe saw the lump in time. I have not explored the prosthetic business in Ecuador, but I would not be surprised if it were quite brisk.

The biggest fiesta in Ecuador is Carnival, marking the period before Lent. It is characterized by drinking heavily and putting your legs out in a road to see what happens. It is also characterized by throwing water at everyone. The water dispensers range from hoses to buckets, water balloons, water pistols, and spitting. The oral form of water dispenser is usually at close range; however, I have seen firsthand some spectacular gushers at several feet. Gualaceo, during Carnival, is a giant wet t-shirt contest, which I am all in favor of, and while it is true that good-looking young girls tend to get the lion's share of the water, there appears to be only slight discrimination. I attempted to take pictures of the Carnival parade, but water and cameras, unless they are underwater cameras, do not do well in close proximity.

The less-than-amusing part of what is mostly harmless fun comes in the form of dousing cars from the roadside or, worse yet, throwing multiple buckets of water on moving cars from other moving vehicles. Kids, both young and old, get into the back of pickup trucks with large tanks of water and drive around looking for targets. If you are said target, you can find yourself driving blind for several seconds under conditions that are prone to produce costly if not fatal accidents. There is an occasional water shortage in Ecuador, and now I know why.

My first major, multiday driving experience took my passengers and me to Baños, a town east of Ambato toward the Amazon basin in the north-central region of Ecuador. Baños is located in one of the most beautiful areas of a beautiful country. The town of Baños is nestled in a valley beneath Tungurahua, the active volcano that surprises international teams of volcanologists from time to time by erupting. The last time it erupted, the volcanologists' equipment was destroyed, so there was no data on just how and exactly what had happened. The eruption sent ash spewing for miles and coated Guayaquil with snow-like debris. Car headlights had to be used at high noon. The town of Baños, the volcano, and the incredible stretch of scenery between Baños and Puyo is a major tourist destination, with good reason. The waterfalls are some of the most spectacular anywhere in the world.

So when Estée's mother and her traveling companion, Nora, a medical student, committed to visit us from Romania, we decided that Baños, the volcano, and the surrounding area would be a great place to take them. We set out on the five-hour trip at a leisurely pace, to the extent that it took us eight hours to get from Gualaceo to Baños. We had reservations at a small and comfortable hotel in Baños and got settled in. Over a simple but tasty dinner at the hotel, we asked the hotel owner if it was possible to get a good view of the then-dormant volcano. "Sure," he replied. "I will have my son be your guide tomorrow. There is a road that you can take."

Excitedly, I played with my camera equipment in anticipation of getting some *National Geographic*, once-in-a-lifetime shots of the volcano. Perhaps it would actually erupt for me and I could catch shots of red-hot lava leaping in the air as I darted around, snapping award-winning "wow" photos.

It did not work out quite that way. We did not start out until mid-afternoon, since our guide was otherwise occupied. The hotel owner's son was in his late teens, a likeable lad who spoke some English. He directed us to an exit from the main paved road that took us up on the side of Mt. Tungurahua. The top of the volcano was hidden in clouds, as it almost always is. Parts of burned-out houses were visible, as well as a swath of former forest that was now ash. That section of the mountain was in the path of the pyroclastic flow that had emitted from the cone of the volcano about a year before. The road got progressively narrower and steeper as we drove slowly up and up. I asked the teenager if it was safe to do what we were doing and he said, "Sure, don't worry about it."

We got to what Indiana Jones might call a bridge, albeit one even he would not consider crossing. This was when I balked. I had visions of all of us plummeting down the side of Mt. Tungurahua and becoming a brief news item on the fourth page of the six-page *Baños Gazette,* titled "Idiot Gringo Drives Relatives, Friends, and Local Boy Off Mountain." At this point and for no particular reason, a false sense of courage overcame sanity and I actually drove over the two planks that were placed slightly crookedly over the washed-out ravine. It appeared that the washed-out ravine was freshly washed out.

Once across the bridge, a very sharp right maneuver was required, at which point we were on a road carved out of the mountainside with nothing but mountain on the left and nothing but, well, nothing on the right. I have no idea how long it would have been before we hit something had we gone off the mountain, but I think we could have had quite some time for conversation before it all abruptly ended. Most of that conversation would likely have been critical of me. The road was so narrow and the mountain wall was so close that I had to fold in the mirror on the driver's side. What was worse was the realization that we had to try to come back the same way. The son of the hotel owner was visibly shaking. I reached over, patted him on the shoulder, and said, "Don't worry about it." We did not go off the mountain, and page four of the *Baños Gazette* had to be content with something probably more mundane, like an article about how stupid it would be to try to drive up the side of Mt. Tungurahua.

Back at the hotel later that night and after a full glass of wine or a wee dram more, Estée and I went to bed. Neither of us slept. Both of us knew that the other one was not asleep, but it was one of those situations in which neither of us wanted to be the one to be accused of keeping the other awake. Finally, the silence was broken and we sat up and talked about how dangerous that really was. My pictures were mostly of clouds and rocks that could be taken anywhere. I did not send them in to *National Geographic*. The lessons learned that day might let us live a little longer.

Road improvement in Ecuador is greatly needed and greatly appreciated when it happens. Roads are being improved all over the country, all at the same time. This generally means that it is very difficult to get from A to B, let alone to C. We have a little circuit that we like to take that goes from Gualaceo through Sig Sig and winds southeast to El Pangui, where we visit our friend Chuck.

It is beautiful country with a large variety of plants, two of which we know by their common names. Chuck knows them all, so it is humbling to be reminded of how ignorant we are regarding plants. After some pleasant days in El Pangui, we usually go southwest to Loja, then turn north and come back home. The road from Loja to Cuenca is being resurfaced with steel-reinforced concrete. The parts that are done are beautiful. The problem is that the transition from resurfaced to not-resurfaced road is not marked in any way.

On a recent trip from Loja to Cuenca, I launched the car off the end of the resurfaced road at just over sixty miles per hour. The drop-off was about two feet and the car went completely airborne. It would likely have been all right if the not-resurfaced road was at least smooth so that some graceful landing could be accomplished, but that was not the case. The car stayed on the road after it landed, but the verbal repercussions by Estée were less than smooth. It started by her asking, "Oh, Wayne, didn't you see that?" and ended with a bout of silence. We now call those moments "Oh, Wayne" moments.

One particularly bad road is the road to Lemon where the buses got stuck. That road is now under construction. It appears that nearly the whole distance is being worked on at the same time. There are fifty-two large dump trucks, life-size versions of the type I used to play with as a kid, that are loaded up many times a day with dirt and rock to be hauled off to a landfill. We are talking about widening and paving a road through mountains, so this is not a trivial task. Dynamite, and lots of it, is required. The road construction crew warned the neighborhood before the dynamiting started. That was on the first day. That was all the warning we got. The frequency of laundry days went up as coffee stains had to be removed from my shirts from the involuntary jerk that my hand made as the dynamite went off during breakfast, lunch, and dinner. The road construction continues with setbacks caused by strikes, poor planning, landslides that include whole or parts of houses, bad engineering, and various other issues related to work hours, pay scales, and the constant breakdown of trucks and diggers.

It is not the fault of the construction foreman, however. He is doing all he can to keep his truck drivers and equipment operators happy. He brought in girls from Cuenca and established a brothel on the roadside about ten kilometers east on the road from Gualaceo. Maria, our house-helper, informed us that the foreman got permission, but from whom we have no idea. I don't think there is a brothel-permit office run by the government, but I may be wrong. Besides, I am not discussing politics in this book. The brothel is located in a white house with a red roof, which I think is fitting. The local wives are complaining since the local husbands are availing themselves of the services even though none of them are working on the road. Fearing that Miguel, our gardener and guard, might follow suit, Estée had a talk with Maria and Miguel about possible consequences of catching a disease, what Estée refers to as the "gift with purchase." Since the establishment of the brothel, work seems to have picked up a little, and the truck drivers that we pass each day seem to smile more frequently. And, well, life and road construction go on.

Now that I have had a few years of driving experience, I recognize that there are many positive signs in our quest to explore Ecuador by car. The roads are improving and other drivers actually let me turn left about one out of four attempts. People we drive past in Gualaceo smile and even wave occasionally as they get to know us. Waving to others on the road is not generally part of the culture here. We do not hesitate to take a trip to the coast and the incredible town of Puerto Lopez where the humpback whales cavort from mid-June to mid-September, or to the Oriente where there are incredible orchids that line the road. We see fewer racing buses, and while there are some reports of horrific accidents, they seem to be slightly fewer in number. I still have not seen the wily red poison dart frog, but that will wait for the next time that Carlos and Marti, and our friends, Dave and Bev, come down. I enjoy driving, and that is a good thing, because it is necessary in our quest for a long and happy retirement in Ecuador.

chapter 5

Construction:
How to Build an Ecuadorian House in Five Thousand Four Hundred and Sixty-Two Easy Steps

For some reason, we never considered buying an already built house. This was possibly a mistake. I think we decided to build a house because we had a vision of where our dream house would be and what it would look like. In our travels around Ecuador, we had not seen any house that tickled our collective fancy. We thought we wanted a Spanish-style country home with courtyards, arches, brick sidewalks, big stone fireplaces, and comfortable rooms to live in and for guests to sleep in for three days (no more). We wanted trees, shrubs, bushes, and flowers to frolic in. There were many times when we thought this dream was silly, impractical, out of the question, and perhaps out of reach considering our budget. But in the end, we actually got many of these things. The description of what transpired in between the decision to build a home and actually moving into the house will take us all on a rollercoaster ride that will take our sweet breath away, leaving our stomachs heaving on a pile of construction rubble.

The architect had a family business and one of his sons was just finishing architect school. He spoke some broken English. That, along with Estée's rapidly improving Spanish, gave us some hope that we would be able to communicate to the extent that we would end up with a house and not a Ferris wheel.

We had a rough idea of elements we wanted in our dream house and the size of rooms. I showed a sketch to the architect and made a few (possibly nonsensical) comments on how he might proceed. Almost three months went by before the architect had time to meet us at the property. He had drawings and we were very anxious to get started with the project. I had visions of pencil drawings on the back of an envelope of how it might look and that progress might be very slow, indeed. Both Estée and I were very surprised when some sophisticated drawings done with a CAD architectural software program were presented to us. One of the sons had taken some pictures of the surrounding countryside and our future house had been dropped by the software into that setting. We were thrilled.

There were detailed drawings of the inside of the house and these needed some serious study. There were only a few changes, but one serious change was required: it was the size and location of Estée's closet. The architect had made a very grave error and had put our closets in the same small room. The size of the room was large by Ecuadorian standards, but by Estée's standards, it would never do. In the end, the architect wisely stopped arguing and enlarged the end of the house to add closet space for Estée. I got the small room. There were a few other changes, but we had close agreement with the overall plan.

Now for the bad news: how much would our dream house cost? The project was divided into phases. The first phase was excavating the site, building stone retaining walls, and putting in infrastructure such as plumbing, drains, and water pipes. Phase two was the construction of the basic house, and phase three included the finishing touches. These were divided into separate costs that had to be approved. All seemed reasonable, so off we went.

Estée and I were back in Chicago when the project started. We requested a lot of pictures and had friends go to the site to give us a progress report. Our absence was a mistake. It was not until later that we realized that the excavation was done by pushing the excess land out toward the river, which not only altered the gently sloping landscape but also buried some large boulders around which we wanted to landscape.

Much of the subsoil that ended up on top of the grassy pastureland was rock-filled clay. Bermuda grass had a difficult time growing in this terrain. Anyone who knows Bermuda grass knows that Mars just might support its growth. It has taken a lot of fertilizer, water, and patience to get anything to grow on our land.

During construction we rented a house in Gualaceo. I stayed to try to prevent any more rock-filled clay from being pushed onto the slightly richer and darker soil that might grow things other than Bermuda grass. Estee continued to go back and forth to Chicago during this time to sell our house (yes, quit laughing). During Estée's absence, Pepper and I were left to fend for ourselves. Pepper was depressed.

My main function was to oversee the building project, which was a joke because I did not know what was going on. Even if I did have some oversight suggestions, I could not express them other than to grunt and point because I could not speak Spanish. At first the workers, all thirty of them, wondered what I was doing wandering around the project trying to look authoritative. Finally, someone told them that this house was going to be mine at some point, but I am not sure that produced the respect I was looking for. I would normally spend an hour or so wandering around, and then get back to the rental house.

During that hour, I would see some amazing things that made me cringe and would make OSHA shut down the project immediately. I have a respect for electricity dating from my childhood, which could have ended abruptly when I put a small screwdriver into an outlet just to see why my mother insisted that I not do so. Having survived that, I am careful whenever I insert a plug of anything into an outlet. So it brought back bad memories to see bare wires inserted into the end of extension cords lying on the ground in the rain and sitting near or in puddles of water.

Workers climbed homemade ladders constructed of thin slats of wood loosely nailed to rotted two-by-fours. It was nothing to see two of these six-foot ladders tied end-to-end with what looked like string to produce a twelve-foot ladder. When brick walls were constructed and scaffolding was required, the boards upon which the bricklayers walked consisted of bouncy bark with just enough wood attached to one side to prevent a nasty fall. There was never a safety rail on the scaffold.

There were nails, wire, sharp pieces of metal, shards of stone or broken glass, and other assorted hazards all about the construction site. Yet, in spite of potential near-death experiences, Pepper and I survived and the construction proceeded with no construction worker deaths that I was told about, although I still eye the cement floors and walls with a tinge of suspicion about who might be encased within them.

As the house took some sort of shape, we were visited by many curious people who wanted to add their opinions to the proceedings. This is very common in Ecuador. Once, when Estée and I needed some documents notarized in Gualaceo, we were surrounded by a dozen residents who examined our documents, our passports, and our conversation as we negotiated the proceedings. Although this is very difficult for Americans to get used to, here it is the norm, so we were not surprised to get these unsolicited visits and opinions at the construction site. One such visitor expressed surprise that the house was only two stories at its highest although it is built on three levels. In Ecuador, the more stories your house has, the more prestigious you are in the community. It is not uncommon to see a narrow, five-story house. As a result of our two stories, we were put into the less-prestigious category.

On one particular Sunday when Estée was in Gualaceo, Pepe and his wife, Ingrid, accompanied us to the construction site. As soon as we got out of the car, a small parade of indigenous neighbors came marching onto our property and silently walked from one side toward the other. When Pepe asked what they were doing, they told him they were following a path to their friends' house to visit. Pepe told them that this was private property and they could not pass this way. They claimed that it had always been a "road" and they would proceed. Estée and I saw no harm in letting them pass, but Pepe was insistent that they go around the property rather than through it, and here we learned rule 421 about living in Ecuador.

If a road or path is established, you, as the new owner of said land, cannot alter the road or path and must make it accessible to any and all. Rule 421 was obviously written by a lawyer. If we had knowingly let them use the path, we would have had to keep that section open from then on. Within days, there was a sturdy fence around our property, and we were ready to move on to rule 422.

As work progressed and phase three started, we were getting excited. The shape of what was being constructed was looking more and more like a real house. Never mind that there were chickens, stray dogs, the occasional frightened cat, and thousands upon thousands of mosquitoes along with an assortment of very strange bugs and beetles in the house. We figured that all these problems could be dealt with later. After all, the architect's son told us constantly, "Don't worry about it." Now it was time to make decisions about paint, tile, wood, grout, stone, glass—just about everything that surrounds you on any given day in a house. In the U.S., it is my understanding, and it has been confirmed by individuals who have built houses there, that you get windows with glass, doors, ceilings, floors to walk on, closets, cabinets in the kitchen—generally a house as a normal person would define it. You can upgrade these things, but they are part of the normally understood construction of a house.

Herein lies the first serious shock of our construction project. These things were not included in the cost estimate of phase three.

"So, do you want a ceiling?" asked the architect.

"I think it would be a good idea, don't you?" I replied through the translation services of Estée.

"How much do you want to spend on the ceiling?" was the next question. "Whatever was in the original plan," was my translated reply.

"There was no ceiling in the original plans, that is extra," was the response. "Don't worry about it!"

This basic conversation was to be repeated over and over as we discussed paint, tile, grout, wood, kitchen cabinets, closets, windows, glass… The list seemed endless and so did the cost overruns. The architect kept assuring us that he was saving us a lot of money by using his architect discount to purchase things. The claimed savings was supposed to match the twelve percent that we were paying the architect to oversee the subcontractors. However, neither the architect nor his sons were at the construction site for days and weeks on end.

Sadly, the architect had a nervous breakdown and spent much of his time in a hospital over the next seven-month period. I truly hope that our project did not contribute to his condition, but it probably did. It fell to us to try to direct the construction and correct the problems as they developed. By "us," I actually mean Estée, since I could not communicate with the stray dogs let alone the workers.

One of the first encounters between the workers and Estée occurred one sunny afternoon as the newly purchased plaster ceiling was being installed in one of the guest bathrooms. We had splurged on some coconut tile as an accent to the otherwise rather mundane tile on the walls. The tile had been installed before the ceiling, and the plasterers were working on the small ceiling.

Estée wandered into the room at the exact moment that one of the workers was wiping the excess plaster from his hands using the coconut tile. Its rough surface was perfect for that purpose. Estée exploded. It was a small explosion by Estée standards, but it was enough to produce some serious fallout. This was one of the few times between hospital stays that the architect was actually on the property. Estée found him and explained the origin of her explosion. The architect bolted in search of the foreman in charge of the plaster detail. Estée and one of the architect's sons, watching from a high vantage point, saw what happened when the foreman got wind of the impending confrontation. He ran around the house, hid behind walls, and ducked into an unfinished doorway. Estée turned to the son and asked, "Should we tell your dad?"

"No," he replied. "This is too much fun."

Other situations were considerably less fun. Of all the subcontractors, the painters were perhaps the least fun. Their attitude was that they were at the construction site to do their own work and their own work only. If some plaster got on the coconut tile, it was not their problem. If some paint got on the woodwork, well, someone would clean it up later, don't worry about it. Estée came around a corner and found one of the painters dipping his brush in a paint can sitting on a tile floor. The paint was running down the outside of the can onto the tile and soaking into the grout that we had paid extra for. She tried to explain that this was not acceptable and the painter should use a drop cloth. She wiped up the paint, got a drop cloth, and placed it under the can. I watched the drama unfold.

As soon as Estée disappeared around the corner, the painter gingerly removed the can from the drop cloth and set it on the tile where he saturated the grout with great globs of excess paint. We will be trying to clean paint for many years to come. At least now my daughter, Sherry, whom we hope will someday live here, will not have to wonder how it got there.

We decided not to build a swimming pool. A friend had one that we could use any time, and we thought we would get more use out of a Jacuzzi, so we built one of those. But how deep should it be? Estée is about 5 ft. 4 in., which is shorter than I, so she was meticulously measured to see how deep the seat should be. A slight error was made, and without a snorkel, Estée has to sit in the Jacuzzi with her nose in the air, making her look like a drowning English aristocrat.

We did decide to build two fireplaces. We had seen many fireplace chimneys in Gualaceo, so we thought this would be a straightforward request. "Sure, we can do that," the architect's son replied to our request. "What kind of chimney would you like?"

"One that is designed so it will draft well," was my hopeful reply.

"Draft what?" was the discouraging response.

"Smoke?" I tentatively suggested. "Smoke from the wood burning in the fireplace."

"Oh, you want a real fireplace!" the architect's son exclaimed. "Oh, we don't do that. Nobody does that."

"What about all the chimneys we see in Gualaceo?" I asked.

"Oh, none of those are real. They are just for decoration. We can look up in a book how to build a real fireplace," he said in a not-very-hopeful tone.

After the real architect was released from the hospital for a few weeks during his bout with another nervous breakdown, we consulted him about the fireplaces. He assured us that real fireplaces could be built and would work just fine. "Don't worry about it." Thankfully, the one in the house works great. The one on the patio works okay some of the time, so we are happy building fires some of the time. Within a week of the consultation, the architect was back in the hospital. I always feel like I played a big role in his setbacks.

Yes, there were many frustrations during the course of construction, such as the workers' habit of opening up all the parts of a faucet, a dishwasher, a light fixture, you name it—then losing half of the parts before attempting to install it. The frustrations of watching a stone worker make a wrong cut in a huge piece of granite countertop. The horrible realization that a very expensive Kohler over-mount porcelain sink has been glued to a piece of granite so crooked that you'd have to stand to one side of the mirror to wash your hands. When an attempt was made to dislodge the sink from the granite to correct the position, the workers chipped the porcelain. The electricians often showed up without ladders or tools to install what parts were left of the light fixtures. The plumbers would show up with no tools or parts and stare at a faucet, presumably to see if they could will it into place. Estée would hand them tools, if we had them, with the understanding that they would put the tools back into her hand when they were done.

This was assuming that the workers showed up at all. Frequently, we would ask the electricians/plumbers/painters/plasterers when they were coming. "We will be there at 9:32 on Tuesday." It seemed that by giving the exact time, they were implicitly agreeing that both they and we knew they would not be there. When we tried to call the contractor at four in the afternoon, we never got a reply. When we'd make contact weeks later, there was always a ready list of excuses. "My cell phone got stolen, I was sick, my car broke down, and did I say Tuesday? I meant next month, I didn't have the parts, and my dog ate the instructions." We found that the excuses were universal; only the contractors changed.

Do these frustrations exist when building a house or during any construction project in the U.S. or in any other part of the world? Of course they do, to some degree. In spite of everything, we have a great house that we really enjoy living in. When we are gone, we look forward to returning.

I love to walk around the house. I try to ignore the random splotches of paint on nearly everything, the crooked sink, the poorly patched, wrong cut in the granite, the extra parts of the faucets, the dishwasher, and the light fixtures sitting in the garage waiting to be installed. We love our house with all its flaws and imperfections. After all, our house is much like me—flawed and imperfect. And Estée claims she loves me anyway. Just as I still love our house.

chapter 6

The Water Association of San Francisco Alto: An Organization Dedicated to the Preservation of Deadly Bacteria and Life-Threatening Parasites in Drinking Water

After Pepper and I arrived in Ecuador in January of 2007, we had about ten days to obtain a car and to get the necessary things to survive in a rental house while our house was being built. Estée and our friends flew back to Chicago, leaving both Pepper and me staring at one another wondering if, indeed, we could survive. After all, I could not speak Spanish and he could not bark Spanish. The local dogs were fascinated by a giant red Doberman playing with tennis balls and stuffed toys in a fenced-in yard, along with the presence of water and food bowls full of water and food, respectively. They lined up at the fence, their collective muzzles dropping open watching Pepper strut around the yard like a thoroughbred racehorse. I heard canine mutterings about the invasion of these foreigners and what would happen to the supply of garbage in general, and bones specifically.

It took a while for Pepper and me to get acclimated to our new surroundings. Pepper spent much of his time going berserk at the cows in a pasture behind us. However, he found a friend in the neighbors' pig. After their first encounter, in which the pig was not put off by the furious barking of Pepper, they both became curious. Many days, they met at the fence to sniff nose to snout. The pig's tail spun in circles and Pepper's cropped tail stood upward, wagging like an inverted pendulum moving in double time. Their friendship was short-lived because a festival came along and *Chancho Hornado* (roast pig) was served. It was sad to see Pepper search and sniff along the fence for his friend.

I spent much of my time going to the construction site and wondering if I should be berserk at what was going on because I do not have a clue what is supposed to go on at a construction site. Our new home was in the initial stages of construction and I could only trust that our architect who was now also our contractor knew what he was doing.

A critical issue at any construction site is water. A lot of water is needed to mix cement and to create pools to sustain chickens, stray dogs, the occasional frightened cat, and thousands upon thousands of mosquitoes. Water is required in the finished house to wash dishes, clothes, and bodies, and to flush things down. I found out that to obtain water, I had to join the Water Association of San Francisco Alto. The Village of San Francisco Alto consisted of eleven buildings, six of which were occupied by people. All the buildings were occupied by stray dogs, chickens, and the occasional pig. It was the closest village to our house and I would be concerned if that was our water source. It turns out that the whole valley is named San Francisco Alto after the San Francisco River that runs through it. Our source of water was a spring high in the mountains.

The Water Association of San Francisco Alto was formed many years ago to build water conduits throughout the mountains to supply bacteria and parasite-laden drinking water to homes in the valley. If you move into the valley, you are required to join the association if you want drinking water containing bacteria and parasites. We know where this water has been. We drink bottled water that is delivered to our house each week. It is not that we are untrusting people; we just didn't trust the water supplied by the Water Association of San Francisco Alto. However, we needed this water, too. We needed to shower and flush and to water plants when the leaves started to droop, so we needed to join the water association. To successfully join the association, one has to be accepted, which suggests a degree of snobbery. To be accepted, one has to cough up a one-time fee of $600 and to attend the annual water meeting. The annual water meeting was where the fun began.

I thought that attending the water association meeting would be exciting even though I did not speak Spanish. It would be an attempt to fit in since we were going to live here. To help understand what was going on at the association meeting, it was suggested that I take an interpreter with me.

Roberto Wilson turned up at the rental house on the day of the meeting and off we went. Roberto turned out to be a charming young man in his mid-thirties who had lived in the United States but found that he could not support his acquired drug and alcohol habits there. He had left his Ecuadorian wife and three children in Ecuador during his foray into the U.S., and now his Ecuadorian wife and three children had left him. The money he initially sent back to Ecuador to support his family dwindled over time and ended up supporting his habits.

This turned out to be a very common story with several variations on the same theme. Many young people, mostly males, leave Ecuador. Their mostly illegal destinations are countries including Spain, Italy, or the U.S., in which big cities like New York, Chicago, and Los Angles are the main destinations. Ecuadorians who are established in those cities help those newly arrived find jobs. Ecuadorians have a very good reputation in the restaurant industry as hard-working, reliable staff. I knew this before Anthony Bourdain confirmed it in his book *Kitchen Confidential*. The intentions of these immigrants are mostly good. They live cheaply, earn money, and send most of it back to Ecuador. Their money is intended to support wives, kids, and parents, buy a motorcycle or car, build a house, and generally create a better life for everybody.

In the area in which we live in Ecuador, there is always a lot of construction going on, and a specific style of house can always be identified as one being built with foreign money, mostly from the United States. Such a house has at least two stories, with a chimney that hints of a fireplace in the living room. These are nonfunctional chimneys and fireplaces, but the appearance is there. The houses are built of cement blocks with a painted cement coating on the front. The sides and back are left as unfinished cement blocks.

It is estimated that at any given time, approximately one-fifth of Ecuador's population is actually out of the country. A significant percentage of Ecuador's economy comes from money sent from abroad. A friend who is high up in the banking industry in Ecuador estimates that about three billion (with a *b*) is infused into the Ecuadorian economy each year. Sometimes the best intentions go astray. Money coming from New York slowly or suddenly dries up and a family is left with no support. The hungry and homeless wife and kids have to move back with the parents and their future is put into limbo, if not outright jeopardy. Now that we are living through a prolonged "downturn," a euphemism used in financial reports on CNN, Ecuadorians, some of the first to lose their jobs in the U.S., are moving back into a bad economy, so there are few jobs to be found. As might be predicted, the crime rate, especially in the big cities, is rising. Roberto was trying hard to avoid the pitfalls of many who had returned to Ecuador, and I admired him for his effort.

The actual village where the water association meetings are held is called Cancai or sometimes Louis Cordero, after the founding father. It is located nearly straight up a mountain east of the location of our new home. Yes, there is a wide, road-like path that goes nearly straight up the mountain. Four-wheel drive is not a luxury going up this road; it is a requirement. Roberto and I arrived ten minutes early. I hate to be late to anything, and at this meeting, I really wanted to sit toward the back. I knew I would stand out anyway, and I did not want to cause any problems that might result in my being rejected by the water association.

As we went up the stairs to the second floor of the tin-roofed conference center in the town with a total population of about one hundred, I noticed that we were nearly alone. As we entered the large conference room, it turned out we were totally alone. There were about four hundred plastic chairs in neatly arranged rows with two aisles. The chairs faced a wood platform with a table and several more chairs.

By the time the meeting was to start, only twenty people were present. This was Roberto's first time at such a meeting, so he was of no help when I asked him to explain what was going on. A half hour later, a few more chairs were occupied and the dais appeared to have the association president and a few other officious-looking people in attendance. Slowly, very slowly, the four hundred plastic chairs began to fill up. Like any meeting, people did not want to sit there waiting for events to begin when there was no hint that events were going to begin. Finally, it appeared the meeting was about to start, a full forty-five minutes late. I was excited because this was my first water meeting, and I was anxious to begin fitting in.

As I surveyed the room, I knew that fitting in was not going to be easy. First, there was the language thing, then there was the clothes thing, then there was the physical appearance thing, and then there was the staring. I am comfortable in front of crowds, but when you have four hundred indigenous Quechua Indians, direct ancestors of the Inca Empire and none of them over 4 ft. 8 in. tall, staring at you, you simply cannot feel all that comfortable. I began to wonder if these were the people that sacrificed their captives by ripping their hearts out. Then I remembered that it was the Aztecs who practiced that form of sacrifice, but did the Aztecs learn that from the Incas or the other way around? It is amazing what nasty little tricks your mind can play, especially when you are ignorant of history. I was stared at since I was the only gringo there, and at six feet tall with white hair and blue eyes, I stood out. I was thrilled when the meeting started because it diverted some attention away from me.

I tried. I really tried to understand what was going on. I rapidly understood that we had started calling the roll. As I heard each name being slowly read aloud, twice if there was no response to the first rendition, my heart sank. After each positive response, there was a pause as the person's presence was duly noted in a ledger. I quickly calculated the time for each response and the number of people present. My posterior became immediately numb, my legs tingled, and the circulation below my waist ceased. Like most people, I am not very patient when it comes to this sort of thing. I thought of more efficient ways to do this, like sign-in sheets, but no. This was the way it had been done since the beginning of the association, or the beginning of time, whichever came first, and this was how it was going to be conducted until the end of the association, or the end of time, which I was hoping would be before the end of the hour. Time may have stood still, but it did not end, which proves once again that there is no such thing as a merciful God.

As more people came in, they were asked their names, and the president went back over the list to find their name and mark it off. We were approaching the H's well into the second hour and I resurrected myself in preparation for my name, Hanson, to be read off. I had the perfect Spanish response, *presente*, ready to speed things along. Then we came to the I's. I looked at my interpreter and leaned discreetly over to ask, "What happened?" He informed me that since I was new to the association, it was likely that I would be the final name.

Plastic is pretty hard to sit on for hours, but these chairs became cement, then titanium. At the end of the second hour, I swear that time had ceased to move at all. It brought back memories of sitting in the Nashua Bible Church as a child of five years old, and constantly, pesteringly grabbing my father's wrist to see that the minute hand had not advanced, at least not as far as I could tell.

By now, the indigenous Quechua Indians had stopped staring at me out of curiosity and instead stared at me more with shared pain and sympathy. We were bonding. Three solid hours evaporated before suddenly I heard something that sounded familiar. Someone said "Robert Wayne" in a Spanish accent, but I still recognized it. I paused for a split second, since I was expecting Hanson to be read out. Before I could respond, Roberto blurted out *presente* in a loud, clear Spanish voice. I saw heads snap toward us and I knew I had blown it. Here I had waited, I wish I could say patiently, but I did not get the opportunity to blurt out *presente* in my best-rehearsed Spanish with a distinct Chicago accent. Now I stared at my interpreter. My part of the roll call came to an anticlimactic end. Quickly forgiven but not forgotten, I was now prepared for a whispered running interpretation of the meat of the meeting.

After the president made some remarks totaling not more than four sentences, there was general chaos, including shouting and expressions of outrage from the gang of four hundred. Then everyone except Roberto and me quickly got out of their plastic chairs, stretched their legs, and pushed and shoved their way to the one stairway leading down to the first floor and out into the dirt parking lot. Roberto told me the meeting was over. The principle outcome of the meeting was that the next meeting was set for the same time next year. I asked what the shouting and the expressions of outrage were all about. The president had suggested that the fee per square meter of water usage be increased. After the shouting, expressions of outrage, and the general chaos, the president wisely suggested that we take this subject up at next year's meeting. This is a sign of a successful and a survivable president. The United States presidents and Congress could learn a thing or two from the president of the Water Association of San Francisco Alto.

As I made my way toward the stairway, I wondered if I had been accepted into the association. Nothing was ever said, so I assumed I had been. I also wondered if I would ever be able to fit in, even a little bit.

Worldwide, water is rapidly becoming a major issue for humankind. One issue is the amount of water available to drink, to wash clothes, to flush things down, to irrigate crops or sprinkle water on grass or petunias. Another issue is what is in the water. I have no desire to grow larger man-breasts from the livestock growth hormones that find their way into the rivers, lakes, and subterranean aquifers.

People are warned that consuming perhaps one salmon a year caught from Lake Michigan would be a good upper limit. Pregnant women should not even look a Lake Michigan salmon in the eye. It is amazing that the number and amount of antibiotics in our water does not render the world free of disease, but that is not the way our world of bacteria works. It is not just the water; it is our food source that lives in the water that adds to the concern. The thought of memory-impairing mercury in the drinking water and in the tuna caught off the coast of Ecuador is—well, I can't remember now, but I think it is bad. Delicious, but bad.

During a trip to Australia a few years ago, I was privileged to meet some remarkable and knowledgeable people associated with the gold mining industry, both in Australia and in Papua New Guinea. I was pontificating in my professorial way about the evils of the gold mining industry in Ecuador, which I was sure had led to the high mercury content in the oceans and thus the tuna, which then led to the warnings by the U.S. government to "just say no" to Ecuadorian tuna fish. My hosts were very kind and intellectually gentle as they told me that some, but relatively little, mercury comes from gold mining. Most of the mercury comes from volcanoes along with a host of other vile pollutants from deep in Mother Earth. My hosts had seen people in Papua New Guinea, mad as Hatters, who drank water and ate fish from lakes fed by streams flowing from or through extinct volcanoes. There were no gold mines to be seen. Who knew? I didn't.

In 2009, Ecuador experienced a drought, the severity of which had not been seen for approximately eighty years. There were rolling blackouts to conserve electricity, which is produced mainly by hydroelectric dams. The Ecuadorian birth rate in 2010 must have gone up, if the famous blackouts years ago in New York are any indication. During times of drought, the Ecuadorians rely on a tried-and-true method to increase the rainfall.

One evening, we were sitting on a secluded patio, looking at the lights coming on in the few houses that are perched on ledges in the mountains at the east end of our valley. It gets dark by 6:30 p.m. all year 'round, but this evening at 10:30, there seemed to be a strange glow in the sky. We walked to the end of the house and discovered to our horror that the side of the mountain south of our house was on fire. We immediately called friends, who immediately called the volunteer fire department, who arrived in force and put out the fire.

We discussed with several friends what might have caused the fire and how dangerous the drought was since all the brush and tall grass was widespread kindling. The fire near our house was reminiscent of the horrible scenes of the California wildfires we had seen on TV and continue to see each year. We were told that the fire was likely intentionally started to produce smoke. The thinking is that since rain comes from clouds, by burning mountains and producing clouds, you can produce rain. It always works because it eventually rains.

I am sure that the people south of us across the river who started the fire were pretty miffed at us for calling the fire department and thus preventing the rain. I am sure because two weeks later at two in the morning, they started another and much larger fire. They figured that we would either sleep through it, or we at least would not bother the fire department at that hour. They were right.

During the drought, we saw many fires roaring up mountainsides, even though the government repeatedly announced that it was a criminal act and that smoke from such fires did not produce rain. It is no wonder that the amount of wildlife was greater in our narrow backyard in Oak Park, Illinois, than in all of Gualaceo and the surrounding hectares.

One morning, our housekeeper announced that she would not be able to work the next day because she had *minga*. I asked through Estée if she had seen a doctor for it, as it sounded like a subtropical disease and we lived in a subtropical location. It turned out that *minga* was a mandatory work detail in which everyone in the water association had to participate. The work entailed digging trenches, laying pipe, cleaning ditches, and generally maintaining the bacteria and parasites in the water supply for the San Francisco Valley and its four-hundred-plus water users. If you did not show up at *minga*, you had to pay a *multa*. That turned out to be a fine of about twenty dollars, and that was a lot of money for most people who lived in the valley.

There are two types of water available to a household in Ecuador. One is *agua potable,* and the other is *agua reago.* As the name implies, you can drink, at your own risk, the *agua potable.* The *agua reago* carries with it extra risk, which is hard to imagine, and while it is drunk by some, it is generally used to water crops and livestock. We have *agua potable* but we do not drink it. However, we use our piped-in water to bathe, brush our teeth, and to flush things down. We have not gotten sick from it yet, and I think it is quite safe for the things we do.

On a Tuesday morning, I turned on the faucet and nothing happened. Odd, I thought. I turned it off, then on again, and still nothing. (Why I thought there would be something coming from the faucet the second time, I can't explain.) It is somewhat similar to being without electricity but turning on the light switch anyway—sheer habit and the disbelief that it is not working. Estée and I went to the cistern that holds several thousand gallons of agua potable. It was empty.

We looked at each other, then up at the road above our property, where there were back-loaders, graders, huge dump trucks, diggers, and dozens of road construction workers. Could there be a link between the widening and surfacing of the road that separated us from our water source and our lack of water? Estée talked to our neighbors, who told us that they had been without water for a week. They were collecting water from the sometimes clean, sometimes muddy water of the Rio San Francisco. It seems that our cistern had given us a week's grace period. Estée asked what was being done to correct the situation. Our neighbors on all sides of us shrugged.

Estée marched up to the top of our property to the road under construction. While she was marching, she called the president of the water association. What was being done about the lack of water for the four hundred people in the water association? Why was this allowed to go on? This was not just an inconvenience; it was a health risk if people had to use river water.

Ecuadorians are not used to dealing with confrontational people, other than those involved in alcohol-induced arguments in bars or on streets. Ecuadorian men especially are not used to dealing with confrontational women, let alone an irate gringa. Estée was pointed to the foreman, whose solution was to leave. He didn't get very far before Estée had him pinned to a light pole. He loosely admitted that, yes, a water pipe may have been inadvertently cut by a bulldozer and yes, the dynamite may have caused a few tons of boulders to be piled onto the water pipe and yes, they really didn't know where the pipe was exactly, now that the landscape had been changed. He did not think that they could get to it this week, or even next week, but he was quite certain that they would eventually get to it, maybe. "Don't worry about it" was his admonition. I am glad I was not there. I could easily have been spattered with blood and been part of the subsequent forensic investigation by the Ecuadorian version of CSI.

I am proud of Estée. She simply, slowly, produced a card that we had been given by the president's chief of staff. Yes, the president of Ecuador's chief of staff. We had met him earlier that year at a function in Gualaceo, and after the exchange of jokes and some interesting conversation (thankfully in English) he gave us his card. He said that if we ever had any problems or issues at all, let him know. We had no idea who he was until we read his card.

Estée showed the card to the foreman and asked him to call the president's chief of staff to explain why we did not have water. We had water early that afternoon. Estée had the admiration of not only the road construction workers who now wave to her as she drives by, but of the four hundred indigenous people in the San Francisco Valley who received much-needed water. News spread like the wildfires used to produce clouds and rain. Estée became, at least for a short time, a legend in the valley. There was talk of nominating her for president of the water association but thankfully, that talk faded quickly.

It is now raining quite regularly. The reservoirs of Ecuador are fairly full for the time being, and it is rare that we flip the light switch without a response. We have not had our water cut off again, so the faucet responds as we assume it will. Whenever there is a two-week period without rain, there is smoke in the air, and that is sad. We are coming up on the next water association meeting, and I am curious to find out whether the president will raise water rates or if she will survive yet another term. I will be *presente* to see what happens, if the bacteria or parasites don't get me first.

chapter 7

Haute Cuisine in Ecuador:
Dining on Children's Pets Named Fluffy

Food and drink are two of the most important elements in our daily routine, along with breathing air and what we politely call our daily constitutional. Breathing we tend to take for granted, but eating is something we think about, plan for, and usually overindulge in. Many people believe that you are what you eat. I firmly disbelieve that tenet because I surely do not eat all that fat that my body translates into the bountiful love handles against which I am constantly waging war.

I was self-consciously aware of my love handles and other bits of fatty flesh as I was laying face up on a massage table on the second floor of our home in Oak Park with nothing but a sheet draped over my oil-covered body. It was a Sunday morning, and a weekly massage was a luxury that Estée and I indulged in. Hanna, a thirty-eight-year-old, medium-built, second-generation German woman was our masseuse. She made house calls to certain clients, and we were privileged to be among them. She was attractive in a masculine sort of way with a powerfully built body and strong arms and hands, coupled with an angelic Germanic face framed in dark-blond hair coiffed by none other than Estée. I usually alternated between near-sleep and a wide-awake state of alert caused by mostly pain, mixed with a small amount of pleasure of some deep-muscle massage.

It was at one of these massage sessions that Hanna introduced some new products that she hoped we would buy and use to the betterment of our health.

The products came in several different types: one was extract of cow uterus and another was extract of cow brain. Hanna explained that Estée could benefit from extract of cow uterus, as the extract, once consumed, went directly to the uterus to strengthen it. Exactly how a strong uterus would benefit Estée was not made clear since she was beyond childbearing age. The brain extract was for me. I, evidently, needed some strengthening of my brain. I was not sure how to take that. I told Hanna that I was hoping for something along the lines of extract of bull penis, but she had that neither in her product line nor in her sense of humor. I would likely have to turn to the Chinese on south Cermak Road for that.

Hanna explained that DNA from the cow brain would go directly to my brain to produce a benefit that I would be proud of—after several months of taking these tablets twice a day at $8.50 a tablet. So for seventeen dollars a day for, say, three months or a total of about $1,500 plus taxes I'm sure, I would notice a benefit. There was no proposal as to how I would know if I received a benefit. Would I take IQ exams before and after? Would I now be able to solve Schrödinger's mathematical equations describing quantum mechanics after I spent $1,500 plus taxes? Perhaps I would be able to calculate the approximations of superstring theory, or even M-theory. Her proposal certainly provided food for thought.

I gently tried to explain to Hanna that digestion did not work quite that way. I explained that your body's digestive system used whatever source of food it got to make amino acids available to turn into proteins in the cell's magnificent mechanism of protein synthesis. If you ate fish, you would not swim better. If you ate an eagle, you would not fly (in part because you would be in jail for killing an eagle). If you ate even excessive amounts of broccoli, you would not turn green. According to President Bush, Sr., you would likely die of broccoli poisoning. The source of food mattered only in that some foods were richer in some elements than others. A small amount of cow brain DNA digested from a tablet was not going directly to my brain, nor was the small amount of cow uterine DNA going to Estée's uterus. If either occurred, it could be very dangerous. I could start to have dreams of grazing in pastoral settings.

Hanna patiently listened, then explained that medical science was way behind in their concepts and their research, and the *doctors*, she sneered, do not understand the benefits of her products. She explained that extracts of many organs could cure diseases, but that medical scientists were blocking that knowledge. She became so insistent that we buy these products to supplement her income that we sadly had to sacrifice our weekly luxury, and we permanently canceled our massages. I have not seen Hanna since, and I miss my mostly pain mixed with a little pleasure.

Estée and I enjoy eating. We plan for it, and we (well, usually I) overindulge in it. As we prepared for retirement, the availability of ingredients was not the first thing we thought of, but it was certainly on the radar. As we researched various countries that were under consideration as retirement destinations, we actually went to grocery stores to see what was available along with what was being sold in the local markets. While researching Ecuador, we were impressed by what was available at Supermaxi, the main grocery store in Cuenca. At first, I approached Supermaxi cautiously because the name conjured up a store devoted to feminine hygiene products, but it turned out to be a well-stocked supermarket. Megamaxi stores, as you might guess, contain more of what is in Supermaxi. Okay, you do not have the choice of twenty-seven different kinds of mustards, and you have to settle for one of a few multivitamin selections rather than selecting from aisle after aisle of vitamins and supplements arranged from A through Z as you can at Whole Foods—what Estée and I refer to as Whole Paycheck—but perhaps that is a good thing.

Beyond the variety of goodies at Supermaxi, the local markets are another source of fruits, vegetables, and surprises. Now all we had to do was to identify what the surprises were. Besides the usual things we were used to buying at the local grocery stores in the Chicago area, here there are fruits called *achiotillo* that look like little red fur-balls, and there are *babacco* and *badea*. There are many different types of bananas, including some small ones called *oritos* and some large, sweet red ones. There are three different types of passion fruits called *granadilla*, *maracuyá*, and *taxo*. There are fruits called *mamey*, *guayaba*, and *guanábana* along with *capulí* and *chirimoya*. *Pitahaya* is a favorite along with *naranjilla*. Ecuador is a veritable cornucopia of unknowns.

Vegetables are a bit more recognizable, but there are some surprises here as well. For example, *achogcha* is a complete unknown, along with leaves of *atchera* that are used to wrap things up before cooking. The corn is nothing like the long, sweet ears we were used to in the Midwest. Here the corn is somewhere near thirty kernels per ear and tough as shredded bits of shoe leather even after it has been cooked for an hour. There is a corn called *mote* that is served as a snack with a hot sauce called *ají*; in fact, almost everything is served with *ají*.

Some serious confusion started when confronted with something as simple as potatoes. Unbeknownst, certainly to me, was the fact that potatoes are native to Peru, of which Ecuador was a part until the 1830s. Peru appears to be of the opinion that Ecuador is still theirs, but that falls into the realm of politics, and I promised to eschew that topic. There is a huge variety of potatoes. We are talking about dozens of types of potatoes to choose from in the market out of the seemingly hundreds of known potato species. I think we could get about four or five types in Chicago. It was truly fun exploring and munching through all the unknowns.

Going to the market on Tuesdays, Fridays, and Sundays is a treat. We are still stared at, but slowly we are becoming known as people who are not carrying guns or knives and who will not give anyone the evil eye. I was given the assignment by Rosa Vintimilla to photograph ingredients and market scenes for her book on the soup called fanesca, a soup that is served once a year at Easter. Photographing people is difficult for me. There are people here who think that by taking their photograph, you are capturing their soul. This is true in several places I have attempted to photograph people, including Papua New Guinea and the Philippines. Estée and I have developed some tricks to try to capture the fascinating faces and the colorful clothes of the indigenous people of Ecuador. Estée will stand as unobtrusively as possible near the subject to be captured and I will make a fuss about exactly where she stands. At the last moment, I will subtly move the camera, snap the picture, and quickly return the focus to Estée. This has worked to some degree. Even if people agree to have their picture taken, it often turns out to be a pose that usually ruins the spontaneity of the moment.

To complete my assignment for Rosa, Estée and I went off to the market to try our luck. It did not work. The women at the market were very aware of what we were doing, and many struck poses that would not work well at all in the book. Their uncanny insight probably comes from the myriad tourists that come to the Gualaceo market to wander around and to try to photograph the fascinating faces and colorful clothes.

Finally, Estée approached several women and told them what we were up to. It turned out that they were happy to have their photograph taken with the hint that they may be in a book on fanesca. This honest approach worked well throughout the market. It was a valuable lesson. After the photo shoot, I printed some photos of the women in the market and Estée and I distributed them. The women were thrilled. It is exceedingly rare that they have any photos of themselves, and they were very grateful.

No matter how well-stocked Supermaxi and Megamaxi are and how many fruit and vegetable surprises there are in the local markets, there are things that we still miss. So once we were settled in Ecuador, we developed what we called the Chicago List: a list of things that we would drag to Gualaceo whenever we went home to visit our family and friends.

As I approached the check-in counter at American Airlines in Chicago's O'Hare Airport on my way back home to Ecuador, I was not only concerned about the accuracy of the meticulously weighed bags but about their bizarre content. They contained mostly items from the Chicago List packed carefully in both the check-in luggage and my carefully packed carry-on bags. I placed one check-in bag on the scale and watched the digital numbers zoom toward the final weight of 51.8 lbs. This was a shock because I had weighed and reweighed the bags, removing heavier items such as the bottle of Rémy Martin VSOP that cost about $40 at Costco but costs $140 in Cuenca, and adding lighter flour sack towels for Estée's use in the kitchen. This kind of packing comes down to priority versus weight. I have had instances at the very same check-in counter at American Airlines where a check-in person had made me remove items with a total weight of a pound and a few ounces and put them in my carry-on bags so the check-in was exactly fifty pounds. If I did not obey, there was the promise that I would be charged an overweight fee, imprisoned, or both.

The attendant taking care of me at the check-in counter this time was busy at her computer. Then she glanced at the big fat number, 51.8 lbs. Our eyes met, and she actually smiled and without saying anything, she removed the first bag and put it on the conveyer belt. The first bag was through. The second bag was 51.2 lbs., and it got the same nonchalant treatment. I was grateful to get a reasonable person for a welcome change. The check-in bags made it through this first hurdle, but that is no guarantee that the contents will make it intact to its final destination.

On a previous trip with bags full of items from the Chicago List, the weight of the bag being removed from the conveyer belt in Guayaquil was closer to twenty pounds than the fifty pounds it started out with. TSA had removed two shock absorbers from the bags slated to replace the worn-out shocks in our car. The shocks were Monroe gas shock absorbers and TSA was concerned that the tiny amount of inert gas was a safety threat to the flying public. Another possibility was that one of the TSA people needed some Monroe shock absorbers. I'm not suggesting—well, perhaps that is better left unsaid. Among other things, rose dust had also been removed; not rose liquid, but the rose dust we needed to destroy all the pests that wanted to destroy all our roses. I was hoping for better this time because I had not packed shocks or rose dust. Still, the content was diverse, with things like printer ink, chewing tobacco for use as an insect repellant, DVDs, selenium, dry cherries and mushrooms, NyQuil, Aleppo pepper, Tom's Toothpaste, smoked Spanish paprika, a Miracle-Gro dispenser, batteries of all descriptions in large packages from Costco, unscented mosquito repellant, and the list goes on and on. How all this might show up on an X-ray is anyone's guess.

I really do have a great deal of sympathy for the hard-working people at America's airports who work for the Transportation Security Administration. Okay, quit laughing! I am one of eighteen travelers who have any sympathy for the 64,000 folks at TSA whatsoever. TSA workers do not have a very good reputation, and like everyone, I have heard horror stories on the six o'clock news of poor judgment leading to inappropriate searches and outright theft in the name of Homeland Security. What do you expect for your almost $10 billion in taxes that pay for the 64,000 members of TSA! So it is always with some slight degree of anxiety (or a little more!) that I approach the checkpoint in any airport. This was the case on this particular day, as I was partially bent over from the weight of my carry-on bags.

My heartfelt sympathy for the members of the TSA stems from dragging the items on the Chicago List through O'Hare airport to be put on a plane that goes through Miami and on to Ecuador. Guayaquil is the final destination where the items on the Chicago List are X-rayed again before entry is allowed. The final insult—I mean X-ray screening—is to look for items such as guns, missiles, cigarettes, bottles of hooch, and crocus bulbs. Yes, I have actually had crocus bulbs taken away.

On this particular trip from Chicago through Miami to Guayaquil, I was carrying some especially strange items. Estée makes wonderful New Orleans–style crab cakes, and we cannot get good crabmeat at Supermaxi, or even Megamaxi. Crabmeat was on the Chicago List: one-pound cans of crabmeat from Costco. I purchased six cans. I also purchased Costco's Danish blue cheese and their best feta cheese, along with bags of pecans and black walnuts, which are hard to find anywhere. A large bag of chocolate chips topped off the weight in the carry-on. Anyone who shops at Costco knows that the quantities are not small. I got an insulated bag from Target and a couple of small freezer packs that would fit into the bottom of the insulated bag. I was set to go. Everything fit into a sizable carry-on, but I am quite sure it could not have been forced into that metal frame that is employed by some but not all check-in personnel.

I put my carry-on on the conveyer belt and proceeded to strip for the TSA. My hip replacement precludes a graceful entry into the safe side of the airport, so I always have to be searched by people, X-rays, puffer machines, or whatever new contraption our scientists have devised to insure our safety. I am always worried at this point in time that, as I am distracted by hands moving toward my crotch, someone is pilfering my precious black walnuts.

On this occasion, I was inspected by the new "photo" device, which did not take long and seemed less invasive than the semi-groping that I usually receive. I was back to the conveyer belt in plenty of time to see an older, bald, overweight, heavily spectacled TSA agent squinting at the screen and my six cans of crabmeat. His eyes became huge, made even bigger by his Coke-bottle spectacles, and he started sputtering at another TSA agent.

I was holding up the line, and people did not appreciate it. I heard someone mutter, "Just shoot him," which I thought was rather rude if not extreme. The second TSA agent was a young but seemingly more experienced agent. He calmly took my bag from the conveyer belt and nearly dropped it owing to the weight, which produced a slight but perceptible frown on his face. I frowned as well to match the mood. With gloved hands, he gingerly opened the zippers on each side and peeled back the top of the carry-on to reveal the chocolate chips, then bag after bag of nuts, before getting to the real culprit, the insulated bag containing can after can of crabmeat. I explained that my wife and I lived in Ecuador and we could not find these morsels at Supermaxi. After I said that, I felt compelled to try to explain what a Supermaxi was, but I let my voice trail off to an inaudible puff of air. He did not ask me to repeat it, and I was thankful. He removed one can of the crabmeat and inspected the label. I kept my mouth shut, which is almost always the best course of inaction. He carefully looked into the insulated bag, then put the can he had in his hand back into the bag. After the bag was run through the X-ray machine again, the young TSA agent did a wipe test on the can. Much to the disappointment of the older TSA agent, it passed. I started to mouth "na na naaa na na na" at the old fat bald TSA agent, but I caught myself. I knew he would love to take my crabmeat away, not to mention my nuts—and we are not talking black walnuts here. My carry-on was reassembled and, amazingly, I was through with my crabmeat and nuts intact.

We portion out those things from the Chicago List that make it to Gualaceo. We try to be generous and share the goodies with our friends Pepe and Ingrid. They, in turn, are very kind to us and invite us often to Ecuagenera for special occasions or when they have American or other English-speaking tourists. On these occasions, we get to taste some of the traditional Ecuadorian dishes. One such dish is *Cancho Hornado*, or whole roasted pig. Ecuagenera was having an early Christmas dinner for all its employees, and a large pig was a requirement to feed nearly seventy people. A traditional food plate includes chunks of pork topped with a crunchy caramel-colored piece of skin. Rice is a must along with *mote*, or corn. Potatoes, salad, and some kind of dessert finish out the feast.

Alex, a twenty-six-year-old Ecuadorian who had recently had facial surgery to repair a nasal septum that had been destroyed in a motorcycle accident, sat beside me with a few leaves of lettuce on his plate. The *Cancho Hornado* was particularly succulent that day, so I was curious why Alex was eating only a few leaves of lettuce. He explained that his doctor told him during his post surgical instructions that he could not eat pork for three weeks. The doctor explained that elements within the pork would inhibit wound healing, and his incisions and his internal nasal repair would go for naught. I nearly spat out a chunk of delicious, if slightly fatty, pork shoulder. Had I missed something so obvious in school? Was I unaware of a recent finding? Alex could not explain the reason, nor did I expect him to. I really wanted to get to the bottom, or at least the pork rump of this.

Later in the week, as I was feasting at a Christmas buffet at the home of Berta Vintimilla, former co-owner of the awarded restaurant Villa Rosa in Cuenca, I asked the surgeon and chief of SOLCA, the cancer hospital in Cuenca, Dr. Raul Alvarado, if, indeed, pork inhibited wound healing. He nearly spat out a piece of delicious and healthy omega-3 oil-infused smoked salmon. He assured me that I had not missed anything in school, nor had I missed any recent information pertaining to pork-induced inhi-bition of wound healing. Raul had no idea how that rumor had started, but it had become "common knowledge," and many physicians in Cuenca completely believed it. He advised patients in his post-surgical instructions to eat whatever they wanted unless they had been subjected to surgery involving the gastrointestinal system, including the gall bladder; then he advised them to eat soft and low-fat foods for a couple of weeks. That is just common sense.

I spent the rest of the evening grazing through the buffet of rare roast beef with horseradish sauce, the aforementioned smoked salmon with capers, the great-wound-inhibitor roast pork with a cranberry chutney, thinly sliced roast ham and chicken breast, at least eight different types of freshly baked breads, seven different cheeses, including a fresh cheese served with a thick compote of figs, and a dazzling variety of desserts. The best wines available were served along with spirits and punch. As the evening wore on, I had the opportunity to engage almost everyone at the party in the pork question. Almost everyone confirmed that, yes, indeed, you absolutely could not eat pork if you had had a recent surgery. Now I was curious if other types of meat such as Fluffy had anything to do with wound healing.

My first encounter with Fluffy was at a dinner at Ecuagenera. I had heard of the seemingly barbaric consumption of the cute little creatures that many American kids had in cages in their rooms, creatures that Mom fed daily and whose cages got cleaned out occasionally by Mom when the smell became noticeable. These cute little guinea pigs had names like Fluffy, Louie, Curly, or something similar. My daughter's guinea pig was named Fluffy.

So it was with both a sense of curiosity and some disgust that I set eyes on a skinned, roasted, head-still-on, whole guinea pig, called *cuy* in Spanish, placed on a platter in front of me. I thought of Fluffy and what my daughter, Sherry, would think. I am moderately adventurous when it comes to tasting things, so I had no qualms about tasting Fluffy. Estée and I had eaten scorpions in China and sea slugs in Japan, so how bad could it taste? I had been told that your first taste of guinea pig was the most important. If it were not a well-prepared guinea pig, you would hate it forever. Unfortunately for me, fortunately for the herds of cuy, this one was not well-prepared. My first bite was mostly fat, which conjured up thoughts of how a big fat rat might taste if I were shipwrecked and starving. I discreetly placed the fatty contents of my mouth into a napkin and faked a few more tastes of guinea pig before faking a full feeling. My first experience of savoring children's pets named Fluffy was over, and it was not a good one.

Months went by and, unbeknownst to me, I was to have a second experience munching on another Fluffy. This experience was at the Paute weekend home of Patricia Vintimilla, the other co-owner of Villa Rosa. The guinea pigs were raised on the premises, so we are talking fresh here. The guinea pigs were skinned, gutted, and skewered before they were placed over an open fire. They were basted with a secret solution of herbs and spices. I expected a short, white-haired, bearded Ecuadorian colonel to show up at any moment. When lunch was served, *cuy* was optional alongside chicken and, of course, delicious if slightly fatty wound-inhibiting pork. I ventured another taste of Fluffy, and this one was a completely different experience. It actually tasted good and not like rat or even chicken. It was more like roast rabbit, yet another common pet in America. What was becoming of me? I was rapidly getting into the habit of eating kids' pets and, well, they tasted pretty darn good.

So why are *cuys* not consumed in America? I would guess that it is the same reason that cats are not roasted and eaten in America. But wait! Perhaps *cuys* are consumed in America!

Arnold Schultz, a friend of our veterinarian who had helped him obtain a job in a pet shop, had clerked in the store on North Avenue and Cicero, on the far west side of Chicago for three years, two months, and four days. He even knew the hours and minutes. This was not his favorite job of the three he had since graduating from Skokie High School. He had liked animals since he was a small child, so he responded to the ad in the *Reader* and the interview with the owner, Juan Jimenez, had gone well. The recommendation of our veterinarian, Marla, helped greatly. Juan had emigrated from Ecuador eleven years ago and was anxious to try a non-Hispanic employee, hoping that Arnold would be more reliable. He tried to give Ecuadorians a chance, but few wanted this type of job. They were much more attuned to the restaurant business and many Ecuadorians also worked in the Chicago Loop as parking valets. In both cases, the pay was much more than Juan could offer. Arnold had missed only a handful of days and Juan was generally happy with his employee. Arnold was looking forward to getting another job in a non-Hispanic neighborhood, since someone with the last name of Schulz didn't fit in very well. However, he enjoyed working with Maria, the Ecuadorian cousin and other employee of Juan.

It was Maria who spotted a peculiar pattern of purchases. All of a sudden, there seemed to be a run on pet guinea pigs. The most peculiar part was that young to older adult males, without kids in tow, were coming into the store to feel up, size up, and purchase guinea pigs. She mentioned this to Arnold who, after paying attention to purchases for a while, confirmed the pattern. Usually, kids were allowed, even encouraged, to pick out their own pets. It gave them a sense of responsibility—at least for a few days or weeks until Mom took over the feeding and the cage cleaning.

Maria was suspicious. She expressed her concerns to Juan. This pattern continued to the point that Juan had a difficult time keeping up with the demand. He mentioned this at a family gathering and was horrified to learn from his relatives that Juan's guinea pigs were ending up on the table of many Hispanic homes as roasted *cuy*. He was informed that Ecuadorians, Peruvians, and Columbians were going to pet shops to purchase *cuy* until the owners of the pet shops became suspicious and stopped stocking guinea pigs. A part of Juan understood, but another part had become Americanized to the point that he saw these guinea pigs as pets. He knew that if this got out, it would make for some nasty publicity. He didn't know how, but it did get out. The *Chicago Tribune* ran an article on the purchase and consumption of Fluffy. Chicagoans were outraged and further purchases of guinea pigs had to be registered, names of purchasers taken, and warnings given. Restrictions were placed on the number of pet Fluffys that one could buy. I am sure that the breeding of Fluffys in the Chicago area has increased greatly over time.

Culinary habits are hard to break. This was confirmed to Estée recently as she stood in line to mail a package at a local courier service in Gualaceo. The person in front of her had a package to mail to New York. The package contained two pounds of fresh cheese and two cleaned, cooked *cuy*. I hope it went air express. Unless the fur is dyed, green is typically not a good color for *cuy* meat.

Food safety is, or at least should be, an issue for everyone. Few people would eat green *cuy*; however, an amazing number of people eat street food that may be minutes away from green. By street food, I do not mean food picked up from the street, although I have seen that happen in Jamaica (the same person also tried to sell me a rock he picked up in front of me). Vendors of food prepared alongside busy streets can have a safe and thriving business and the food can be tasty. On a typical Saturday noon in Cuenca, one could observe the elite and not-so-elite either walking or driving up to get a plate of delicious, if slightly fatty, pork with a mashed potato patty and *mote* (corn). Salad would likely be part of the plate along with the ever-present rice. Ketchup was served along with mayonnaise. Other options might include *cuy* and some kind of fried fish. Upon closer inspection, however, safety issues might come into focus.

As I was deciding if this was something I really wanted to try, I saw that the little paper cups of mayonnaise had a dry crust on top and were sitting in the sun with flies parading around the rim and taking an occasional foray into the white body of the condiment. A particularly persistent puppy was licking the top of the reservoir of ketchup stored under the cloth-covered table. Other dogs in various stages of starvation with obvious skin and oral hygiene issues were also on the scene. The potatoes were being mashed with an unwashed beer bottle in preparation for the tasty fried morsel of a small patty mixed with cheese, one of my favorite things when prepared under more sanitary conditions.

I am shocked that Cuenca hospitals are not full of near-dead people and Cuenca morgues are not full of really dead people, sick or killed by unknown microorganisms. That they are not is a testimony to the durability and the adaptability of humankind. Forget all about wound healing. I am sure that many local residents and tourists have great experiences eating street food and most seem to survive. I am just as sure that some unsuspecting local residents and tourists get Montezuma's revenge, the Texas two-step, or whatever euphemism that particular set of local residents or tourists use to refer to explosive diarrhea; but if death does not ensue, some consider it worth the risk to experience the culinary delicacies of the country. Suddenly, eating Fluffy did not seem so out of the ordinary. Now I was curious about health-care in Ecuador.

chapter 8

Healthcare in Ecuador:
Please Do that Voodoo that You Do So Well

On a warm, windy, late-summer's day in Oak Park, with fluffy white clouds moving rapidly across the sky forming patterns of fanciful animals that brought back early childhood memories, I was sitting in, perhaps, the worst place in the world—the one place I hated more than any other place, and the one chair I hated more than any other chair: the dental chair. Each time a visit to the dentist was required—almost never an option, but required—I broke into a sweat. Then I actually went to the dentist. I was a firm believer in the rhyme that Ogden Nash penned, "…some tortures are physical and some are mental/But the one that is both is dental."

The bad memories of my dental experiences began as a child, as they do for most people. While I loved my father, and while I had a great relationship with him over his short lifetime, I hated his profession and everything it stood for. He was a dentist—my dentist. I developed the usual number of cavities most kids of my time did by gnawing through mountains of candy and gum, even though I was encouraged more than most kids not to. When the necessity arose, which it inevitably did, I was taken to his office.

The smells and the sounds of a dental office are unique. If you blindfold me today and walk me toward a dental office, I will know at a great distance away, and I will resist. There was the distinct smell of cloves, which I actually liked, but every time I smelled cloves in the apple cider around Halloween, I thought of my dental experiences. When I smell cloves now, I think of my father and now I can smile. There was the wafting odor of disinfectant mixed with a hint of cigarette smoke. I was not supposed to know that my father smoked. He was never allowed to smoke in the house, resulting from my ultra-religious mother's fear that seeing him smoke would instantly lead my older brother and me directly into a life of sin that included smoking, according to the gospel of my mother.

I was never allowed to actually see the gospel according to my mother, but I was assured that it matched the older gospels with a few additions that were designed to correct the rather liberal parts of that Bible. That, I was assured by my mother, was all I needed to know. I ended up sinning and smoking anyway, and I am sure that my mother blamed my father for all my many sins and my years of smoking. I supported that view because otherwise I would have to take responsibility.

I started smoking when I was twelve. My other sinning started a little later. I was accepted into an experimental math and science program at the University of Northern Iowa in Cedar Falls when I was twelve. This was a summer program in which all students were required to take math courses, but one could choose physics or biology. Since all the girls chose biology, the choice was obvious. I chose biology, too. How else could I learn how to sin?

On top of the biology classes, we had to choose a research project. I remembered at ten years old sitting in a physician's office reading the end table literature and waiting for my mother's physical check-up to be over. The literature was produced by the American Cancer Society and spelled out the dangers of smoking. This was 1955. There were photographs of the pathology of invasive lung cancer, which impressed me greatly even though I had no idea what I was looking at. All I knew was that smoking was a bad thing according to adults, so when I had to choose a research project, sorting out the evils of smoking seemed like a reasonable, if optimistic, choice.

First, I had to design a smoking machine to extract the tar and nicotine. This machine was a rudimentary aspirator hooked to a sink faucet. The suction nipple was linked via a rubber tube to a glass tube with a series of holes lined by soft rubber. The cigarettes were placed in these holes, lit, and the faucet was turned on to create suction. The machine smoked twenty cigarettes at a time and a V-shaped portion of the tube collected the vile-smelling tar. I spent days with my smoking machine. It did not smoke the cigarettes evenly, so some burned down to the nub more quickly than others. If I removed one, the suction on all the cigarettes was broken, so I would replace one and then light it. I soon discovered that it was more expedient to light one in my mouth and have it ready to replace any spent cigarette. I started smoking.

The university sent me home after the summer was over with my smoking machine and cases of cartons of cigarettes. There were thousands and thousands of cigarettes. My father had built a simple laboratory in our basement, so I had the space, the means, and the excuse to continue to smoke and to dream of sin. So when I went to my father's office for dental work, I clearly recognized the faint waft of cigarette smoke.

The pulsating whirring sound of the drill bit making short precise passes in and around the enamel of a diseased tooth is a sound that will make most people tell their innermost secrets. Before my father got the newest obtainable water-cooled high-speed drill in the fifties, the slow drill was all that was available. The slow drill was invented during the Spanish Inquisition and was used to great success by the Grand Inquisitor, Torquemada. Okay, perhaps I cannot document that, but I am absolutely sure of it.

Once ushered into my father's dental chair, X-rays were used to identify the offending tooth, or teeth, and the slow drill, initially hidden from my sight, was cleverly slipped into my mouth. "This will only hurt a little," was the often-heard phrase. I was young, but I knew the word "bullshit." I steadfastly refused Novocain. I would grip the vinyl-covered chair arms with the superhuman strength that would choke a large boa constrictor. My father would beg me to use Novocain, but in my mind, the thought of what I knew to be a foot-long needle plunged savagely into my gums with the pain that it must produce was far more frightening than that little, slowly rotating drill bit.

One day, the amount of work needed to repair a tooth was extensive and seriously pain-inducing. My father told me that he would not do the work without Novocain. He assured me that I would only feel a little pinprick and that it would not hurt. "Bullshit," I thought. He told me that if I refused the Novocain, I would have to go to another dentist. I seriously considered it but thought that at least I could try to get even with my father if he lied to me. Getting even with an unknown dentist would be more difficult. He told me to close my eyes and open wide. After a minute went by, I told him to go ahead and give me the shot because my jaw was getting tired holding my mouth open. I heard him chuckle. "I gave you the shot a minute ago," he said. "Did it hurt too much?" I was genuinely angry to think I had suffered—*really* suffered—for years, brought about by my ignorance and misconceptions of the foot-long needle and the pain that the needle must inflict on poor children worldwide.

Years later in Oak Park, as I once again sat in the worst chair in the world waiting for the dentist, all the smells, the sounds, and the fear flooded back into my mind. Dentistry had changed a lot since my father's days of practice, but many of the smells and sounds were the same, and I still tried to choke the boa constrictor with my steel grip on the chair arm.

The dentist in Oak Park was aware of Estée's and my plan to retire to Ecuador. He wanted to get all the dental work done for both of us before we left. We joked about jungle dentistry and mused on how they might administer Novocain in the Amazon Basin. I shuddered. "Perhaps a Novocain-tipped dart from a blow gun" I offered, having read about the combination frog skin poison and *curare* that indigenous Waorani people used on dart tips to hunt monkeys and other food sources in Ecuador. After I contributed that comment, I didn't think it was very funny, and the cubicle fell silent for a few moments as both our minds wandered in different directions. When conversation returned to the cubicle, we made tentative plans centered on future trips back to Oak Park to maintain our dental care without the use of Novocain-tipped darts. I paid the $685 for the check-up, X-Rays, one filling, brief visit, and left.

A few months after arriving in Ecuador, I felt a twinge—an oral twinge. I instantly smelled cloves, the faint waft of cigarette smoke, and heard the slow grinding sound of the instruments of the Spanish inquisitors. I would tell them anything and everything. I would make up subversive stories and conspiracy theories they wanted to hear. I would name names. The twinge went away for a day, but it came back with a vengeance and made the transition from a twinge to a throbbing, then a stabbing pain. It was clear that I was not going to make it back to Oak Park and the relative safety of my familiar dental cubicle. I needed to find someone, anyone, with a Novocain-tipped dart. I needed help!

In the many trips Estée and I made to Ecuador, we made friends. We now called on those friends to recommend a dentist, but not just any dentist, one who was the best dentist in all of Ecuador. Indeed, the best dentist in all of South America north of Patagonia and south of where the FARC were kidnapping people in Columbia. We thought we could limit our search to what was in between. I was willing to travel. They recommended someone who was thirty-five kilometers away in Cuenca. Okay, it was convenient, but was he or she good? I was assured he was. A call was made, and he could see me right away. I assessed and reassessed the level of pain to see if this was really necessary, and it was.

I was somewhat reassured by the familiar smells and the sounds upon entering the dental office. I heard the nearly inaudible high-pitched scream of a modern drill, a sound that is eerily similar to the much louder Russian jet engines on the Hungarian Malév airline Estée and I flew years ago from Belgrade to London. I thought I smelled a hint of cloves but no cigarette smoke. I was ushered into a cubicle and as I sat down, I gripped the arms of the chair and heard the air go out of the boa constrictor. A kid—I am not kidding around here—a kid came into the room. I almost bolted. I wanted an older gentleman or a gentlewoman who was actually old enough to have gone to dental school. Was this kid the dentist who our friends had recommended? Yes, indeed, it was. Then I remembered over the years how each successive medical school class that I taught looked younger and younger. It didn't necessarily strike me each year, but perhaps once every three years, I would see some exceptionally young-looking face that reminded me that I was getting older.

The mere baby, Fernando, really had gone to dental school. Beyond that, he had done two years of post-graduate studies in Colombia (the country) on oral reconstruction and dental implants. I was amazed. He probed and prodded a few minutes, then I heard the familiar "ahhhh, there is the problem." X-rays were taken, and when he re-entered the room, he said with confidence, "You have an abscess under the base of one of your crowns. The crown was not properly done. It does not fit under your gums far enough. We will have to remove the crown and redo it properly." My confidence in Oak Park dentistry dropped like a monkey hit in the carotid artery with a frog skin poison/*curare*-tipped dart. The abscess was drained, pain relievers were prescribed, and appointments were made to correct the sloppy and high-priced Oak Park job. After the final appointment when the beautiful, if that is possible, new crown was fitted, I paid the grand total of $265 for everything and drove home. On the way home, the topic of conversation was about why people were leaving the United States in droves to have dental and medical procedures done overseas. At least from my dental experience, I would recommend Dr. Fernando Vega to absolutely anyone.

Medical tourism is on the rise worldwide. Follow the money! I was sitting at lunch in Chicago with Dr. Jim Thrall who was chief of radiology at Harvard Medical School. We were discussing changes in radiology, and the discussion migrated to the fact that CT scans and MRI images were being sent via computers overseas to be evaluated, then the results were sent back the next day. The cost of having these medical images evaluated was a fraction of the cost to have an American radiologist look at the same images. The American College of Radiology was up in arms over the implication that a radiologist in India might do an adequate job of interpreting CT scans and MRIs. This is an exact analogy to the loss of jobs in many industries in America. Yes, follow the money. Medicine is no exception.

Nora, our friend and sixth-year medical student at the University of Azuay in Cuenca, was recently approached with a job offer to help guide English-speaking people coming to Ecuador for medical tourism. These are people, mainly from the U.S., seeking medical procedures not covered by insurance. These procedures are usually cosmetic in nature (or against nature), such as breast augmentation or facial restructuring. Medical tourism has existed in Mexico and other Latin American countries for years. As the insurance crisis in the U.S. grows, people will be coming to countries all through South America for medical issues beyond cosmetic procedures, such as hip replacements and cancer treatment options. Ecuador is not going to be left out.

After I retired to Ecuador, I had an opportunity to test the feasibility of having my hip replaced in a still-foreign country. If I decided to have my hip replaced in Ecuador, it would be somewhat akin to what a medical tourist would have to go through.

It had been years coming. Slow, degenerative diseases are like that. They take their sweet time as they slowly eat away at discs and joints and brain tissue. I was happy that my left hip was the issue, and not so much my discs or, to my knowledge, my brain. Hanna, with her cow brain extract, would argue the point. I first noticed my hip pain when I began to lose at tennis. My friend and neighbor, Larry Pelka, started beating me—first occasionally, then frequently. I had nothing else to blame but my hip. Neither of us took losing well; we still don't. I went through a period that I refer to as my McEnroe period in which I would throw tantrums, storm the net, yell and scream, and slam my racquet. I resented the fact that I did not have ball boys or girls, lines people, or an umpire to abuse. I would then pick up what was left of my shattered and disfigured racquet and sulk home. In retrospect, Larry was very tolerant of me during that period and I thank him for that. I bought amateur but fairly expensive racquets in the few-hundred-dollar range, so my tantrums became quite expensive over time. My temper was completely restricted to the tennis court, and I always confessed my need for yet another new racquet to Estée. After a while, she suggested that I consider buying disposable Bic racquets and sign up for anger-management classes. In retrospect, I see that Estée was very tolerant of that period in my life as well, and I thank her for that too.

During one tennis-court moment, it was not me but Larry who flung his racquet. He obviously learned that from me. I looked at him in shock and felt ashamed at how my behavior had looked to him. In later conversations, we dubbed that behavior "raging against aging," but we both rejected anger-management classes as something totally unnecessary. I also found out that Bic does not make tennis racquets.

Over several years, my losing continued but my rage subsided. I began to experience pain climbing stairs and going down stairs. We had a lot of stairs in our three-story, narrow English Tudor–style house—four counting the wine cellar in the basement—so there was a lot of pain. By now I was retired and our plans to go to Ecuador were in full swing. I was certainly not in the mood or inclined to have hip-replacement surgery. I was willing to put up with a little pain. Just how long should one wait to have a hip replaced? This is not an easy question.

In conversations with Dr. David Fraser, a friend from Canada, I was told that in the Canadian system, surgery was put off until it was considered absolutely necessary, whatever that means. In many people who wait too long for surgery, the muscles surrounding the hip and in the leg deteriorate from disuse. If it hurts, people will compensate by simply not walking unless it is absolutely necessary, and that is usually to the bathroom and the kitchen and perhaps the wine cellar. The recovery time, Dr. Fraser told me, was a very long and tedious process in people who wait too long. He knew. His seventy-four-year-old wife had undergone a hip replacement, and he was waiting for a knee replacement. He was seventy-six years old. His advice: Don't wait too long. Contrary to his advice, I put it off for a long time.

We were back in Ecuador, and it was Estée's fifty-third birthday. We had a very quiet celebration at a local restaurant and resort called Uzhupud, which means "hot pepper" in Quechua. It was a Tuesday night, and we were alone at 8 p.m. The manager was a young and friendly thirty-two-year-old man named Daniel. He joined us for a glass of wine, dessert, and interesting conversation, very thankfully in English. After learning that we were not tourists, and that I had some association with cancer research, his comment was, "Oh, you have to meet my aunt Rosa; she does volunteer work for SOLCA, the cancer hospital in Cuenca."

Months went by and we ate at Uzhupud several times. Each time, Daniel reiterated the necessity that I meet Rosa. After several more months, Estée and I hosted a dinner at Uzhupud for twelve people. They included the president and several professors from the newly formed University in Gualaceo. I heard the door burst open, and I heard, "No, Aunt Rosa, don't do it." Then I heard the infamous, "It's okay, don't worry about it."

Suddenly, a six-foot, not-very-petite woman surrounded by a presence that exuded confidence mingled with a hint of danger was standing next to me with her hand extended. The table fell eerily silent. All conversation ceased. Forks with food on their way to mouths, or empty on their return trip to the plate, froze in space and time. The normal busy clatter of a meal being consumed ceased. All eyes turned to Rosa. Given the reception of those around the table, I was not sure if I should stand, shake hands, give a kiss on each cheek, as is the custom in Ecuador, or if I should genuflect while giving the sign of the cross. After shaking hands, Rosa went around the table and received the greetings of the others. It was obvious that this was someone who garnered a lot of respect. I was particularly interested in the interaction of the university president, Juan Cordero, and Rosa. He was the former minister of education in Ecuador and a bit of a presence himself. I saw the respect he had during his greeting, and from that, I knew that Rosa was not to be trifled with. After her greetings were completed, she plopped herself down beside me, ignored everyone else, and we started a friendship that continues to this day.

Slowly at first, forks began to move again, the normal noise of dishes and glasses clanging against the table and each other started up, and the meal resumed. After our disjointed conversation was over and we made plans to meet again, Rosa jumped up, kissed me on both cheeks, and waved to the table on her way out. A hush fell again, and one of the professors, Carlos, said in a reverential tone, "Oh my god, that was Rosa Vintimilla! I was in love with her years ago, but I never had the courage to ask her out when we were young. She was way out of my league. I have not seen her for years, but she is still beautiful." Everyone nodded. Daniel apologized profusely as he presented me with the bill for dinner, not for the size of the bill, but for his aunt's behavior. I assured him that it was no problem, and I was glad we had finally met.

From that day on, Rosa was insistent that Estée and I join her often at her weekend home in Paute. Rosa noticed that I was limping as we walked around the garden, and as we talked about getting older, we both agreed that it was better than not getting older. I told her that, at some point, I would have to get my hip replaced. She immediately began giving me advice, which is Rosa's way, but I paid attention. If Tina Fey had not written the book *Bossy Pants*, Rosa could have. I still had not thought about the possibility of having the surgery done in Ecuador—that is, not until I met Dr. Wellington Sandoval.

Estée and I were invited again to Rosa's weekend home for lunch. We were told to come at one o'clock, and we arrived at 1:15, which is hours early for Ecuadorians. If you are told to come for a lunch at one, you will be the only one there until a few others start to show up at 2:30 to 3:00. Now we know to ask if they mean Ecuadorian time or American time.

Rosa had told us that she had a special friend she wanted us to meet. As we drove down the lane to Rosa's house, we saw a very large military presence. There were troops on foot, some on motorcycles, and others in armored personnel carriers. The hub of activity appeared to be Rosa's house. We wondered what trouble Rosa had gotten into now. Estée and I entered and found ourselves with Rosa and her brother-in-law, Edgar. The special guest had not arrived yet. We sat and chatted for about fifteen minutes, then two gentlemen came in, one in a major's uniform and the other in a suit. A few minutes later, in walked Wellington Sandoval and his wife. Unknown to us, Wellington was the minister of defense for Ecuador. Given the bad luck that had befallen the previous ministers of defense, it was a good idea to have some guards present.

Wellington and his wife were charming and entertaining. He was a cardiovascular specialist in the military and former director of the Metropolitan Hospital in Quito, by far the largest and best-equipped hospital in Ecuador. He had stepped down from that position to become minister of health for Ecuador in April of 2005. The health issues of the military and the police had been part of his ministerial duties, and both branches had come to know and trust him. So, when the minister of defense position became available for the third time in five months, the heads of the military and the police successfully argued that Wellington was the right man, and he assumed that position in August of 2007.

During lunch, he and I discussed the possible reasons for the very high incidence of stomach cancer in Ecuador, along with Chile and Costa Rica. The incidence is almost as high as Japan, with the highest incidence being in South Korea. It can be assumed that the incidence of stomach cancer is high in North Korea, too, but it will be a long time before we know that little tidbit. After lunch, and after some prodding from Rosa, who had known Wellington for years, Wellington told us the story of the plane crash of 1965.

Wellington was twenty-four years old at the time of the accident. He had just completed his medical training in the military. He was a lieutenant, soon to become a captain, and was on a military flight crossing the Andes toward the Pastaza Airport with nineteen passengers on board. It was September 16, 1965. Wellington was sitting in the rear seat on the left side of the plane by the aisle. After all, he was the lowest-ranking officer on the plane. Everything was routine in the old DC3 transport plane, which was renamed the C-47 by the Ecuadorian Air Force. The hum of the engines caused everyone to nod off with their thoughts going in all directions. It was very stormy in the Andes, as it frequently is.

Suddenly, the engines were abruptly throttled up, first to a roar, then to a scream, as the plane desperately tried to climb almost straight up. The DC3, an old workhorse during WWII, was a reliable plane, but it was not designed to climb almost straight up, so it didn't. It crashed into the jungle about twenty miles from the airport in the vicinity of Puyo and Fatima. The tail and then the rear part of the belly were the first parts to hit the treetops, then the undergrowth, then the rocks and earth. The tail section broke off, stopped abruptly, and spewed its contents forward, ejecting Wellington and three other officers into the undergrowth. The rest of the pieces of plane continued for a short distance and burst into flames. The trees, the undergrowth, the rocks, and the earth tore the plane into different-sized fragments as the plane ripped a swath through the jungle. The burning, twisted metal of what were once beautiful wings, an intact body, and two large and powerful Pratt & Whitney engines became a funeral pyre.

Amazingly, Wellington was conscious. He remembers crawling away from the burning carnage, first to the right, then the left, to avoid being burned by the flaming debris of the thousands of parts of the plane and his fellow passengers who were ablaze around him. After a long time, the horrific sounds of the crash faded away, leaving only the sounds of the crackling fires. Wellington was left with the smells of burning fuel, the smoking contents of the plane, and smoldering, charred flesh.

A short time after the crash, military helicopters hovered over the still-burning site. Rescue workers were on the scene. It was not very hard to find because smoke rose high above the jungle. Rescue personnel injected morphine into Wellington's upper thigh and gently placed him on a padded, flat board. They carefully tied his chest and waist to the handles on the sides of the board to avoid putting pressure on his two deeply cut legs. They wedged his jacket around his head to stabilize his broken neck, and tied a band across his forehead. His upper cervical vertebra was fractured, and a little below that, two vertebrae had crossed over one another. Under most circumstances, he would be dead, or at best, a quadriplegic. His jaw and his left hand were fractured. A signal was given with a wave of a hand, and the board started its assent to the rescue helicopter. Search and rescue personnel scoured the mountainside, then they scoured it again. Wellington was the only survivor.

The first few words that came out of my mouth were broken. I stopped and started again to say, "That is amazing," then thought how stupid it sounded to say anything. What can anyone say after that story that makes any sense at all? Wellington broke the silence to say that he had recovered completely and believed that his life from then on took on a special meaning. He thought then as he does now, that he must have a higher purpose in life, that he was spared for a reason.

It became apparent several months after that meeting at Rosa's that being minister of defense was not that higher purpose at the moment. The FARC crossed the line, which happened to be the northern border of Ecuador, and in the ensuing conflict, FARC computers were confiscated, the contents of which revealed government dealings that those governments did not want revealed. It was a pre-WikiLeak leak. Wellington lost his job, or at least that job, but he was promptly posted to Buenos Aries as the Ecuadorian ambassador to Argentina. Not bad duty, but I am not discussing politics. Since then, Wellington has retired, and is living with his wife in Cuenca.

As the former director of the Metropolitan Hospital, Wellington had formulated opinions of who could do surgery and who could not, as least not very well. He recommended an orthopedic surgeon he knew who would do a good job replacing my hip if I decided to have the surgery done in Ecuador. After all, what could go wrong? It turned out that, in this case, unlike our move and the construction project, not much. I went to Quito with Rosa, and we met the surgeon for an evaluation. New X-rays were taken and his immediate comment was, "Wow, that must hurt. Why did you wait so long?" I could only shrug. He consulted his appointment book online and we set up a date. The surgery would be done on a Thursday and I would be out of the hospital by that weekend, barring complications.

On Wednesday morning, Rosa, Estée, and I waited in the boarding area to fly Tame, the Ecuadorian airline, the forty-five minutes from Cuenca to Quito. Rosa was busy greeting almost everyone in the waiting lounge. We had been with Rosa enough in public to know that she apparently knew almost everyone in Ecuador. We boarded the plane first when Rosa explained to the airline personnel that I was nearly crippled and needed some extra time to board. They looked at me suspiciously but did not want to tangle with Bossy Pants. As people boarded the plane, she was like a queen greeting her subjects. Rosa held court. After we got settled in, I asked Rosa how it was possible that she knew so many people. Rosa was, at one time, the secretary of social security of Ecuador. In that position, she got to know a lot of people.

We checked into a hotel not far from the Metropolitan Hospital and I checked into the hospital for my final tests and briefings before Thursday morning. During the check-in process, Rosa, after greeting her physicians and staff friends in the hospital hallways, rejected my first room as not having a view that befitted my eyes. She asked for a room that had a view of Mt. Cotopaxi, thinking that if it erupted, I would have something to occupy my time. I got a room with a great view, and if you twisted your head a little and looked between buildings, you could, indeed, see Mt. Cotopaxi on a clear day. We had no clear days, but I was assured that it was there.

I have a fatalistic attitude when it comes to surgery. I have a little advantage in that I know the risks. I know anatomy because I taught it in medical school and I know surgery to some extent because my degree involved research into tissue compensation following surgical procedures. I slept well. Thursday morning came and went without me knowing much about it. I was assured later in the afternoon that everything went well. The surgeon had to add almost two inches to my left leg to make up for the bone and cartilage I had worn off the hip joint. The pain in the joint was immediately gone. I still had pain from the surgery, but I knew this would go away with time and patience.

The ratio of nurses and hospital staff to patients in the U.S. is about one nurse or staff member to ten thousand patients. I may exaggerate a little, but I don't think that ratio is far off. The ratio of nurses and hospital staff to patients in Ecuador is about five to every one patient. I was shocked at the attention I received. It was not just because of Rosa, although her attention did not hurt. The fact that Wellington Sandoval visited me Friday after the surgery did not hurt either. After his visit, I saw nurses peeking around the corner of my door, wondering who the hell I was. I kept the charade up as long as I could. I was out of bed on Friday and taking tentative pain-free steps. All was well. A young and attractive nurse's aide volunteered to go into the shower with me to help "wash-up," but I rejected her help. Estée agreed that the service was just getting too good.

On Saturday morning, the surgeon visited for about twenty minutes, going over the list of what I could do—and, more importantly, what I could not do—following hip-replacement surgery. I could not play tennis or ride horses or even pedal a bicycle. He asked what my plans were about getting back to

Gualaceo. We had tickets to go back Tuesday morning on Tame. He asked about the height of the mattress in the hotel, which was low. After thinking it over, he asked me to stay in the hospital until Tuesday. He would have me taken straight to the airport from the hospital to catch the flight. I saw dollar signs. If you have extra hospital nights in the U.S., you are talking thousands of dollars.

Tuesday morning came. By now, I was walking around the room and in the hall. My tennis days served me well and the muscles in my hip and leg were responding to the exercise. Estée was worried that we had not transferred enough money to our account to take care of the extra days in the hospital. She went to the cashier to pay and discovered that the total for everything was $8,250. Almost $5,000 was for the imported metal implant in the hip. Compare that with the $50,000 to $60,000 bill in the U.S., and that is without the offer of a shower with a pretty nurse's aide. Medical tourism—follow the money.

I was strapped to a gurney by the ambulance personnel and wheeled to the emergency room. They gently hoisted me into the back of the ambulance, which doubled as a taxi for Rosa and Estée. At Estée's urging, the ambulance driver turned on the siren through a few intersections. The airline, Tame, was warned that an ambulance was on the way with a passenger. I was taken to a room in the bowels of the airport where the airport physician met me. I had to be cleared to fly. I then had to get off the gurney onto a wheelchair to go through security; yes, even in Ecuador, you have to do this for internal flights. The terrorists have won. Rosa negotiated the most comfortable seat on the flight, and off we went.

My medical adventure in Ecuador was quite amazing. Usually when people here say "don't worry about it," I sweat bullets, but in this case, they were right. Estée and I have medical insurance in Ecuador. We pay about $450 a month for both of us. It didn't cover the hip replacement because it was a preexisting condition, a phrase often heard in the U.S. We have been healthy since coming to Ecuador. We have the occasional bout with amoebae, and we have to get medications for parasites once in a great while, but either they are getting used to us or we are getting used to them.

We were getting things together to drive to the jungle again, one of our favorite things to do in Ecuador. Miguel and Maria, our helpers, do a great job taking care of the house and our dog when we are gone, so we feel very comfortable taking off for days or even weeks. On this occasion, Maria looked a little worried. She told Estée that when we got back, we needed to have a look at Miguel. He did not seem healthy to her. He had lost weight and was drinking copious amounts of water both day and night. We were gone for three days, and when we got back on a Sunday afternoon, indeed, Miguel did not look well. We pay medical insurance for both Miguel and Maria through the social security system in Ecuador, so on Sunday evening, we all drove off to Cuenca to the social security hospital and the emergency room. Nora, our adopted medical student from Romania, was with us, and she helped us negotiate the labyrinth of rules and regulations. We got to the hospital at 8:30 in the evening, and I was sure we were looking at a 1 to 2 a.m. return trip to Gualaceo.

Miguel's blood glucose was 365mg/dl. The normal range is from about 60-110 mg/dl. You don't need to be a physician to know that we are talking about a serious problem with blood sugar. More blood tests were conducted, and it was established that Miguel had type II diabetes. He was hospitalized until Friday while his metabolism was stabilized. We were home in Gualaceo by 11:30 that evening; not bad. The biggest problem was to convince Miguel that he could not eat and drink anything he wanted. The two-liter bottle of sugar-laden cola each day was out of the question. He has, with Estée's encouragement, insistence, and sometimes threats, done very well. However, he constantly expressed his desire to be truly cleansed so he did not have to take a pill every day. To be truly cleansed, he wanted to see a shaman who could perform a purification ritual. We convinced him to stick with the daily pill ritual and watch his diet, but I was curious. Could a shaman really cleanse and purify me in ways I was unaware of? Perhaps a purified body would make me more perky and brisk in the morning.

I reluctantly slid my body toward the edge of the bed, swung my legs toward the floor as my torso and head moved upward in a less-than-coordinated motion of getting up in the morning. I've repeated this motion many thousands of times, but it still comes as an unwanted intrusion on a usually pleasant night of dreams. I had some coffee and continued to wake up while staring at the mountains at the end of the San Francisco Valley in which we live. After an unknown amount of time and number of cups of coffee, I showered to face the day scrubbed and clean—or that is what I thought until I met Lourdes.

Lourdes is a beautiful, highly intelligent English professor at the University of Azuay in Cuenca. She also knows people whose profession it is to clean you beyond what you can achieve in a shower. We are not talking about nurse's aides volunteering to scrub you squeaky clean; we are talking about serious cleansing by trained people, usually women, who perform a *limpio* or cleansing ritual that will leave even your innermost parts squeaky clean. It is a variable but complicated ritual designed to rid you of evil spirits that make you feel less-than-perky on an average day and downright grumpy on a bad day. The evil spirits can be caused by Andean vapors or bad air. They can even be caused by other people's bad thoughts about you, a vestige of the evil eye. So when you are feeling less-than-perky or downright grumpy, you need to get cleaned. I was told by Lourdes and by Rosa that I needed to get clean, really clean, perhaps for the first time in my life. Lourdes was busy with her teaching schedule, so my dear friend Rosa volunteered to introduce me to my first *limpio* ritual.

Off we went to a cement-covered square at 5 p.m. on a Friday evening. As we entered the square, there were over thirty people, most of them with small children, who were standing in a semicircle waiting their turn to be cleansed of evil spirits. I watched the process and it looked harmless, so I thought why not. The ritual took about five minutes for not-very-evil children, so I estimated that perhaps it would take about an hour, maybe a little more, for the evil I had penned up inside me for months if not years. Perhaps my sinning had finally caught up with me.

Rosa introduced me to a spritely eighty-one-year-old woman who has been cleaning people most of her life. She learned the trade from her mother who learned it from her mother. The knowledge of the ritual has been passed down through many generations. It is a tradition that is being lost in recent years, and no one knows what the future holds. There are many variations of the ritual to choose from. I opted for the simplest ritual to see how it would go. By going with the minimalist ritual, I might retain some evil, but I figured I could deal with that later. After all, I had gotten this far in my dirty, un-cleansed body.

After I sat down on a stool about eight inches off the ground, my first thought was how I would get to my feet again without crawling to a metal post that was several meters away and embarrassing myself. After all, I was now the center of attention for the thirty-plus Ecuadorians whose cleaning had come to a screeching halt.

The first part of the cleaning process involved a bundle of herbs and spices that were crushed between the old woman's hands. She placed the bundle over my face and I was asked to breathe in deeply. The smell was fantastic. Perhaps this was the origin of aromatherapy. After a few minutes of breathing in deeply, the bundle of herbs was used to swat me all over. It reminded me of the African potentates with their animal-hair switches they used to shoo flies away in poorly made movies about African potentates. Muammar Gaddafi could not have done so well.

After I was swatted and thrashed for several minutes, the old woman walked to her young assistant and retrieved an egg—not just any egg, but a fresh egg laid by not just any chicken, but a free-range chicken. It is best to call ahead to make an appointment so the egg is waiting. If not, you may have to wait a long time for the assistant to chase down a free-range chicken and procure a proper egg. We were fortunate to have a proper egg on hand. The uncracked egg was rubbed over my body, including my head and eyes. Then I was asked to breathe on the egg. The assistant removed the egg to a corner and broke it into a small glass with the yoke intact, and then water from a plastic coke bottle was poured into the glass. The old woman "read" the egg and water combination and looked at me with a grim face.

I was nervous. Perhaps my previous years of smoking and my continuing years of sinning had produced a body that just could not be cleansed. I was told through Rosa that I had some residual effects of an evil eye, or something like that, but it was not too bad. I had bad air to some degree, but that too was marginal. I was tense and that was quite serious. I attributed that to the fact that I still did not know how I was going to get up from the stool that was eight inches off the ground.

After being helped to my feet, Rosa went through the same ritual, and the thirty plus Ecuadorians went back to their cleansing. The show was over. Rosa had some bad air as well, and she was full of tension. Rosa, according to the old woman, was worse off than I was. I liked this old woman.

The proper way to get cleansed is to repeat the process three times. You are supposed to come Friday, Tuesday, and then end up on the next Friday. Rosa was not happy to see that some of the thirty-plus people were simply going to three different stalls to get the three cleanings out of the way in one extended session. As we walked back to the car to go home, I felt oddly cleaner and strangely ready to sin again. When I entered the house, Estée asked if I had been rolling in the grass. There were remnants of herbs throughout my clothes and in my hair, but even she admitted that I smelled pretty good.

This was the simplest method of being cleansed. There are much more complicated methods, usually done by a shaman. People come to shamans for cleansing and to be guided through a drug-induced ritual to clean the inner soul, usually using extracts of mushrooms or a potent extract of a flower called the Angel's Trumpet from the *Brugmansia* family. The extract called ayahuasca contains mainly scopolamine, hyoscyamine and other tropane alkaloids including atropine. While I am not a pharmacologist, these chemicals sound like they may do more than just clean out your inner soul. After reading that death is one of the common side-effects, I lost interest. If things don't go right, one might hear the angel's trumpet all right. I felt quite clean without taking additional risks.

My education of traditional and conventional medicine in Ecuador was not complete, but it was as extensive as it was going to be until I got sick again. I was hoping that my further education would be a long time away. Is medicine in Ecuador perfect? Of course not. There are, however, similarities between the practice of medicine in Ecuador and what is going on in the United States and other industrialized countries. Good medical care exists both here and in those countries, but it does not exist for everyone. It is available to a select group.

Americans and Europeans are extremely arrogant when discussing medicine in their respective countries. I know the system too well, and I know that the medical system is not good for many of the uninsured or the under-insured, and that is after Obamacare kicked in. There are untold millions of people in the United States alone without insurance. And for those with insurance, the cost is extremely high. My daughter works mainly for health insurance because her husband is self-employed and insurance would cost them nearly $2,500 a month for a family of four. Did I say we pay $450 a month for both of us? Medical tourism—follow the money.

Ecuador has a social security health system, but getting treated there is not a simple matter. I see a large number of older indigenous people limping in an all-too-familiar way. They are in desperate need of the replacement of one or both hips and they cannot afford the surgery. In many cases, they do not know the system. They do not have the help or the support to even know how to go about having their hip replaced. They do not have someone to ensure that they have a view of Mt. Cotopaxi while they convalesce in their hospital room, and certainly no one to get into the shower with them. I wince every time I see that limp because I know the pain. Follow the money.

chapter 9

The Premature Death Certificate: Enough Said

Her name was Maria Margarita. She lived on a mountain named Turmolon near the village of Cancai, high above and a little north of Gualaceo. She appeared to be very old, but no one knew exactly how many years had passed in her life as a Quechua Indian. When asked, two of her daughters, Maria Juanita and Maria Jesus, answered with a range from ninety-two to ninety-five years old. The consensus of her five daughters—each named Maria-something—centered on ninety-three. Her four sons had little to no interest in their mother or in her age. If I had to guess when I met her, I would have thought I was being kind to give an estimate of one hundred and five.

The lines of her toothless face looked like the complicated street pattern of downtown Chicago viewed from atop the John Hancock building. She was probably four feet, nine inches at her zenith, but when our lives met, her hard life had rendered her to four feet, five inches standing as straight as possible, which was not very straight. Carrying huge bundles of hillside clippings for the *cuy* on her small back was one of her self-imposed daily duties. Raising nine children and cooking mostly rice for breakfast, lunch, and dinner—sometimes with bits of chicken parts or a small fatty piece of questionably fresh pork— provided the family sustenance. The main diet of rice was supplemented with food purchased with the money from the sale of milk from one cow, eggs from six chickens, and two pigeons, sold for twelve or sixteen cents, respectively, at the market. Add to that the housekeeping, including sweeping the dirt floor of the small four-room crumbling adobe house and doing whatever maintenance was needed, which kept her very busy. Her husband, although never officially made such, had not graced the cloth-covered doorway for a time long since forgotten. It was thought, but never confirmed, that he had died of severe alcoholism years ago.

A roasted *cuy* was a once-yearly treat at Christmastime or, more likely, Carnival; but that was only if times were good. Otherwise, the *cuy* that were not stolen or had not died from one of numerous infections were sold for several dollars at the Sunday market. This rare windfall was usually converted into rice, and so the food cycle continued. A singular joy she had each day was feeding a mixture of soupy rice, a small amount of quinoa, if available, and sometimes leftover maize from the night before to the four "Indian" dogs. Clearly, she made sacrifices to provide food for them. Their fat bellies, silky fur, and adoration of their master were very unusual among the slowly starving, mange-ruffled, flea- and worm-infested, ill-tempered dogs that are the sad norm along the streets and roads of Ecuador. All these chores were routine during much of her life, but as ageing took its toll, manifest outwardly by her bent back and her severe limp, various chores were dropped, and now life was mainly centered on day-to-day survival and making sure the dogs were fed.

One dark cloud that hung over much of her life that was more sporadic than the daily chores, but much more serious, was trying to protect her one-third hectare of steep mountainside land from the constant thieving attempts of strangers, neighbors and, most frequently, relatives. Not only were the products of the crops stolen, which were usually corn or potatoes, but also on more than one occasion the poles demarcating the outline of the property were moved inward to increase the land holdings of the neighbors. These thieving ways have produced a litigious Quechua society in which everyone knows and is likely to use lawyers on a weekly to monthly basis.

Life is hard for most of the Quechua Indians in the Andes of Ecuador. Thirty-year-old women can look old here. If a girl is not pregnant by the time she is seventeen, she is looked on as one who may have the curse of being barren, and that truly is a curse among the Quechua. The Quechua are one of many indigenous Indian tribes that were in the area long before the Spanish arrived over five hundred years ago. They are descendants of the Incas, and their spoken language of Quechua is grounded in the Inca language of runa simi.

Years of descending in the morning from her home at 8,600 ft. to Gualaceo at 7,000 ft. and back home again in the evening, repeated sometimes three to four times a week along steep dirt paths on dry days and more often, treacherous rain-soaked mud paths, resulted in a spectacular degree of arthritis. Her right hip was badly in need of replacement. Her arthritis and especially her right hip could be featured in Robbins and Cotran pathology textbooks and taught in pathology courses throughout the world.

The fruit and vegetable market in Gualaceo is open every day, but the main market days are Tuesday, Friday, and Sunday. Her attendance at market days was long past, and she missed those days and the friends she saw at the market more than anything in her life. Long ago, she was prevented from making the long trek by the extraordinary pain in her hip. Her right leg was now bent outward so that her right foot unevenly touched the ground at a right angle to her other, more normal foot. The facial expression of pain at each step was only partially hidden by the narrow-brimmed Panama hat she always wore. Her awkward stance was hidden to some degree by the brightly colored, heavily worn orange skirt called a *pollera* with a once-white decorative boarder at the hemline and a blue blouse with lace. A faded brown shawl topped off this ensemble, along with worn-out black shoes that slipped off when she was able to take a few steps. These were her dress clothes, worn to mass on the few occasions she was taken to the Catholic church in Gualaceo, or on special occasions, like going to the hospital.

At two o'clock on a Tuesday afternoon, the old woman collapsed to the floor in her adobe house where she lived with her fifty-seven-year-old mentally challenged daughter named Maria Rosa. She had not been well for some days and was short of breath and sometimes dizzy. The daughter could cook and do light cleaning, and that was her duty for many years. Unfortunately, she was mentally challenged enough to think that her mom was asleep on the floor, despite her awkward position with her arm twisted behind her back. Her breathing was shallow, coming in wheezes and whispers. Maria Rosa sidestepped her for more than two hours. Maria Jesus, another daughter of the large parade of sons and daughters, happened upon the scene.

A small circus developed slowly at first, then with increasing fervor with all the attendant hubbub as other sons and Maria-something daughters were apprised of the situation. One of many Gualaceo-based Toyota pickup taxis was summoned to the mountains by cell phone to carry her to the hospital in Gualaceo. She was gently placed in the backseat. She was so short that there was room for her to stretch out and for Maria Jesus to sit comfortably by her head. The others sat in the front or piled into the bed of the four-door pickup.

Dr. Jose Garcia was the attending physician on that Tuesday afternoon and the first person in the Gualaceo regional hospital to see Maria Margarita. Dr. Garcia was a twenty-four-year-old recent graduate of Cuenca University Medical School. He was four months into a mandatory one-year public-service stint and felt lucky to be assigned to tend mainly to the indigenous in Gualaceo. He was only thirty-five kilometers east of his family in Cuenca and felt very fortunate that he had not been assigned, like most of his classmates, to some remote area in the Oriente like El Pangui or the even more remote area around Coca where the fearsome and unpredictable Waorani tribe lives along the tributaries and main channel of the Napo River. At least here in Gualaceo, the hospital was equipped with simple but new equipment, which made routine medicine well, routine for the most part.

The still-unconscious old woman was carried into an exam room in the one-room emergency section of the single-story hospital. Cleanliness in this hospital is nearly impossible, owing to dust from the dirt streets. Many tiles on the floor of the emergency room were broken and dirt replaced the missing pieces. The walls were desperately in need of fresh paint to replace the faded moss green color that now looked as if it were an unintended faux finish. The black-haired nurses dressed in almost-white, over-starched uniforms scurried around Maria Margarita. She slowly became semiconscious and could respond to simple requests like "move your arm over here." A measure of her weight and height would have to wait. Her blood pressure was in the high normal range and her breathing was rapid, shallow, and labored. Her heart rate was high, nearing ninety beats per minute, and she had a fever measuring 102°. Dr. Garcia ordered a plane film X-ray of the chest, which revealed moderate to severe bilateral opacity of the lungs. She was suffering from pneumonia. Pneumonia is the actual cause of death in many elderly and is the terminal event in the course of many diseases. Two-a-day doses of an antibiotic was prescribed and she responded well.

This is where Estée and I came into the story. Okay, it was mostly Estée. We became involved because Maria, one of Maria Margarita's daughters, works for us. After we encountered the other siblings, we came to regard her as the gem and the genius of the family. She and her common-law husband, Miguel, have been working for us for nearly seven years. Maria does house chores four hours a day and Miguel works outside in the garden during the day and watches over the place during the night, protecting us from mostly imagined threats. Occasionally there are people who have no business near the property who run off when Miguel shoots his camouflaged double-barreled 16-gauge shotgun, hopefully toward nothing that will get us thrown into jail. Over the seven years of their employment, Estée and I have come to appreciate their honesty and their loyalty very much.

They have a love of animals beyond most people of any country, especially those in Ecuador where the appreciation of animals is purely utilitarian. Without her knowing it, I once watched Maria sitting on the ground with two-week-old chicks surrounding her. She picked up each chick, whispered something to it, and finished with a little peck on its beak before returning it to the ground. The thrilled little chick would scurry to the end of what seemed like a line of waiting chicks with the hopes that this could be repeated, and usually its wish was granted. The two Indian dogs that are on our property are no less well cared for. Perhaps Maria learned the love of animals from her mom's loving treatment of hers.

To round out the dog foursome on our property, we currently have a male Doberman named Squire and a new female Doberman named Sabrina. Tragically, our precious Doberman, Pepper, who we brought from Chicago, died from a rare blood cancer. The two Dobermans dwarf the Indian dogs and use them as sometimes willing stuffed toys. One of the Indian dogs, Tarzan, is a stay-under-the-bed-pretty-much-all-day kind of dog, so he is rarely seen. This leaves a pack of three to guard the perimeter, which they do with simulated ferocity. Because of our good relationship with Maria and Miguel, and because of their love of animals, we have no hesitation leaving our house to explore and photograph the wonders of Ecuador.

It was without any sense of inconvenience that Estée and I volunteered to use our Ford Explorer to go to the hospital to pick up Maria Margarita and bring her home to recuperate in our casita where Miguel and Maria live. When we arrived at the hospital, a small- to medium-sized circus was in progress. One of the myriad in-laws was taking charge of any and all situations as they went fleeting past the constantly changing scene. She was a tall 5 ft. 1 in. woman in her fifties, and she had a mean and nasty continence in her most jovial of moods. This was not one of them. She was busy making it abundantly clear to all relatives in attendance and to strangers in the vicinity that Maria Margarita was coming up in the mountains to convalesce with her.

Then she met Estée and her plans derailed into a train wreck of what for her was of historic proportions. I think she instantly saw that Estée was more than her match. Estée loaded a conscious but still not ambulatory Maria Margarita into the back seat of the Explorer, and as the circus continued with all the accompanying flourishes and less-than-graceful acrobatics, Estée explained, with feet planted squarely on the ground, that Maria Margarita would have to come back to the hospital a few times. It made more sense to have her stay with us in the casita, which was ten minutes from medical care. Our home was an hour closer to medical care should she need it; otherwise, that hour difference entailed a ride over roads that make the back streets of Chicago after an average winter seem smooth as glass. It is not that the road to our house is paved or in any way better than the road to the in-laws' house, but it is an hour shorter. Our Maria saw the logic in it, so her mom came home with us.

Two days later, I backed the Explorer out of the garage, pulled it to the bottom of the fairly steep walkway to the casita, and watched as Maria Margarita, with a Maria-something on each side, carefully made her way down to the open back door of the car. Her ability to walk even a few steps was a vast improvement. Her eyes were bright and she was breathing well. She clearly had responded to the antibiotics as the physician had hoped she would. She looked a whole year younger; I would say one hundred and four.

Estée had gone to the casita earlier to make sure Maria Margarita was pre-pared. I briefly saw Estée in the house again but did not pay much attention. I noticed as the elderly woman was coming down the walk, she had almost-white socks on with oversized, worn-out black dress shoes. The white socks were in stark contrast to what the indigenous Quechua wear. Again, I did not pay much attention. We drove to the hospital, and Maria Margarita, with her broken gait, shuffled into the waiting room.

It sometimes helps that both Estée and I stick out in a crowd, and this was one of those times, and while Estée stands above the crowd, at six feet with almost-white hair and blue eyes, I get a lot of jaw-dropping responses. It is not that people in Gualaceo have not seen gringos. Gualaceo has many foreign tourists who come to the markets and to visit Ecuagenera. It is just that few tall, white-haired, blue-eyed gringos are seen helping a diminutive ninety-three-year-old indigenous woman in a Panama hat and white socks through the crowded narrow halls of the Gualaceo social security hospital. While I am used to being scrutinized by students in medical school classrooms, and by audiences in lecture halls while giving seminars in radiation oncology, I still felt awkward walking Maria Margarita down the hall. It was a feeling similar to the beginning of the water association meeting with four hundred indigenous people gawking at me.

After she weighed in at a fully clothed 41 kg (90 lbs.) and was found to have a normal temperature and blood pressure, it was time to see Dr. Garcia. This entailed another long, limping shuffle down a people-packed corridor. She kept losing her right shoe, the shoe on her foot that was at a right angle to the front. Estée's quick and logical solution was to remove the shoes and let her walk on her almost-white socks. We got her to a bench in the open-air waiting room and, with a lot of effort on everyone's part, got her seated. I sat beside her and we smiled at each other off and on. The other people in the waiting area looked at me, then at Estée, then back at me. I looked at the wall, at the ceiling, and then I glanced around the room.

Suddenly, I realized that the people in the room were not looking at me any longer. Their focus was on Maria Margarita's feet. My gaze followed theirs to the mostly white socks, which were so out of place. I then realized that most of the mostly white appearance came from a black pattern on the socks. She was wearing Holstein cow print socks that Estée had supplied her with earlier that morning. The socks were a gag gift to Estée, and I am sure she had them stored unused for years. How the socks ended up in the containers bound from Chicago to Ecuador remains a mystery that only Estée can explain. She might have worn them to a Halloween party at our friends in Bartlett, Illinois, or in Council Bluffs, Iowa, but it was very unlikely she would have worn them in Gualaceo. Suddenly, I felt that I was no longer the one who stood out in this crowd.

Probably out of deference to Estée and me, Maria Margarita was seen by the doctor ahead of everyone else. No one seemed to mind. They just sat with their mouths open, staring at the Holstein-cow-print socks. We were ushered into an office that doubled as a storage room. There was an old gunmetal gray desk and two black metal chairs with cracked padding on the seats and arms. Estée and I stood. Dr. Garcia listened to Maria Margarita's heart and chest sounds, tapped on her back over the lungs, and was pleased by the normal tympani and at her overall progress. The next and last visit was to be in four days on a Monday when another chest X-ray would be taken. She was to stay on antibiotics until then. She also stayed at our casita.

The next Monday arrived. I was very busy thinking about studying Spanish. I was thinking of using my Rosetta Stone software and my Logitec ear phones with a microphone to tell precisely how far off my pronunciation was. Since I was so busy thinking about all this, Estée agreed to take Maria Margarita back to the hospital for her final check-up while I thought about how busy I might become. At the last minute, I decided I could put off my self-study Spanish lesson until later. Procrastination, especially as it pertains to learning Spanish, is something I excel at. I once again became the chauffeur. As usual, our Maria, along with Maria Jesus, was in attendance. Maria Margarita passed her check-up with all normal values, and her chest X-ray showed clear lungs. A comparison with the first X-ray was not possible because that one was lost in the system.

When the exam was over, our Maria raised her head to Dr. Garcia and in a diminutive but clear voice asked, "Is this where we get the death certificate?" At this moment, Dr. Garcia was thinking of moving things along because he had hours of time to spend with other people in the packed waiting room and on the benches, and those standing in the hall, all hoping that, indeed, things would move along. He clearly did not think that he had heard Maria correctly. His expression was one containing a kind smile beyond his youth combined with a quizzical frown. This combination is not an easy one to acquire on one's face, and it produced a comical expression that lingered for an inordinately long time. Before Dr. Garcia was able to untwist his face and coordinate his thoughts concerning what he thought he heard, Estée uttered an astonished, "¿Qué?"

Without blinking, Maria simply repeated her question: "Is this where we get the death certificate? It would make it a lot easier and it would save us a lot of time when she dies." This time, Maria Jesus nodded her approval of the question and both waited for a response. Now, our Maria had clearly thought things through. It would, indeed, speed things along if we all had our signed death certificates tucked away. Once the grim reaper had paid her visit, the end game would be greatly accelerated. Our surviving relatives would simply present the signed document with date and cause of death filled in. It is a pity that it does not work that way. The possibility of fraud springs to mind, along with first-degree murder or at least homicide (perhaps justifiable homicide in the case of disagreeable family members).

Maria Margarita is stone deaf, so as long as she could not see our Maria talking, she was content to smile and look straight ahead, anxious to leave. Dr. Garcia's mouth opened twice to begin a cogent response, but both times it closed again because the response he had in mind did not match the question. All Estée could think of to say that came close to matching the question was, "But, Maria, she is not dead!" Dr. Garcia, recovering but still with a quizzical look on his recently well-exercised face, quickly confirmed that indeed "she is not dead."

The follow-up question by our Maria was only somewhat less inappropriate. "When she dies, is this where we get the death certificate?"

Estée composed herself. "Maria, Dr. Garcia takes care of sick, but living, people. You have to look into a death certificate later; hopefully, much later."

By this time, Dr. Garcia had regained part of his composure and the urge to move on had taken hold of him once again. He thanked Estée for being able to think of something to say and gave her a knowing smile when everyone else turned toward the exit. He graciously ushered the mini-entourage out the door and moved on to the next of what seemed like hundreds of patients. We returned Maria Margarita and her Holstein socks, now hers to keep, to the casita and thought of ways to return her to her home once we were sure proper care was waiting.

This would be a nice ending to our true story with Maria Margarita recovering, the premature death certificate put on hold, and everyone moving toward their previous state of mind and effort in their daily lives. But alas, no, this is not the end of our story.

Even though we were not in attendance, the moving circus of relatives was in full swing with more clowns and dancing bears with tutus than ever. The mean daughter-in-law had literally kidnapped Maria Margarita's mentally challenged daughter while her mother was fighting off pneumonia in our casita.

We then learned that the mentally challenged daughter was claiming that our Miguel had raped her. At first, Miguel did not take this too seriously, but it was suggested to him that he should do so. In Ecuador, there is a twenty-five-year minimum jail term waiting for those convicted of raping a physically or mentally handicapped person. Once this was explained to Miguel a few times, then a few times more, he started to take the accusation more seriously. He was informed of the possible consequences of a conviction by the same lawyer who was contacted to make out Maria Margarita's last will and testament to deed her land to Maria Jesus, who would take care of the mentally challenged daughter. All of a sudden, the last will and testament took second ring in our three-ring circus. Miguel took center ring and center stage within the ring.

A few days later, a fourteen-year-old nephew of our Maria named Segundo, meaning second in Spanish (if you can imagine the psychological damage associated with naming a son "second"), climbed the mountain and talked to his mentally challenged aunt. She informed him that the mean sister-in-law had threatened to beat her if she did not maintain her story of being raped by Miguel. Upon discovery of this conversation by the mean sister-in-law, Segundo was also threatened with the same treatment. We were flabbergasted to discover that everything—the desire to take care of Maria Margarita, the last will and testament, the kidnapping, the accusation of rape, the threatened beatings—were all centered on one thing: LAND. We discovered that among the indigenous Quechua Indians in the Sierras of the Ecuadorian Andes, land trumps life. We suggested that perhaps all the land issues would get sorted out, and that perhaps Maria Margarita's health should come first. What a concept! We think that our Maria agreed.

A few days after that, Maria Rosa, the mentally challenged daughter, was found wandering around the mountainside and our Maria was alerted. She had escaped the mean sister-in-law but did not know what to do or where to go. By the time we heard of it, she was in our casita, and it was starting to get dark. We told Maria and Miguel that she could not stay in our casita overnight. Maria and Miguel told us that it was okay because Miguel was innocent of the rape charges. I do not think they understood why we were so insistent that she leaves now! Here we have on our property the plaintiff and the defendant in a rape case in the same house, and planning to stay together overnight. We asked them to call the lawyer immediately to confirm our insistence that she leave right away. He informed Miguel and Maria that the woman must go.

That disaster was averted, but what will be next? Our friends, who wonder what we do from day to day in our retirement, have frequently asked us, "But don't you get bored?" Not for a moment!

Later on, we took a healthy Maria Margarita back to Mount Turmolon to her home where she will be looked after. Poor Miguel may be collateral damage, but we think he will escape the accusation of rape. We are assured that he has a good lawyer who is looking into all the angles. We also think that Maria Margarita will live until she is one hundred and five years old, so that she at least looks her age. When she dies, all that will need to be done is to actually get a valid death certificate, and to complete the date, time, and cause of death. Premature death certificates are still not being given out in Gualaceo.

chapter 10

Expats in Ecuador:
From the USA (and a Few Other Places) with Crazy Love

Vilcabamba, a small lazy town in southern Ecuador, is famous for several reasons. First, people who were born, raised, and stayed in Vilcabamba tend to live a very long time. It is one of several communities worldwide that has been studied to determine the reasons for their longevity. It could be genetics, the food, or the water—perhaps the lifestyle or some combination of these. No one knows. Second, the area around Vilcabamba produces Ecuador's finest coffee, which is promptly exported before it has a chance to grace the breakfast tables in Ecuadorian homes. (Instant Nescafé is the preferred coffee beverage there, thanks to the power of marketing.) Third, Vilcabamba is the home of some of the first true nut cases to immigrate to Ecuador from the United States and from a few other countries as well.

To define someone as a nut case is to pass judgment that may seem unfair. After all, I am sure that some people, no matter how unreasonable they might be, would lump me into that category. However, I have no qualms about labeling some behavior as nutty, and the people who exhibit that behavior as nut cases. I have been to many places in California and to Sedona, Arizona, and I have seen them. It is not that these are the only two places nut cases exist, but those are the places where I have encountered them in large numbers. Walking along the crafts tables in Sedona, among the magic necklaces, the healing bracelets and the vortex-inducing and soul-transporting crystals, I remember two young women conversing. "A little to the left," one said to the other, "I think I can feel the vortex over here." Estée chastised me, and not just a little bit, for snickering a little too loudly.

New Year's Eve leading into the year 2000 brought out some of the strangest human behavior around the globe. People in Vilcabamba built bunkers to live in during the coming near-total destruction of the earth. Exactly how bunkers in Vilcabamba would protect people was not explained. The proponents of Earth's destruction during the millennium transition have a bit of egg on their collective faces since nothing happened.

I am sure, but I can't prove it, that those same people shifted their doomsday attitudes to fit the new threat: the end of the Mayan calendar. Many books and the movie *2012*, based on the end of the Mayan calendar, vied for the honor of producing even greater levels of strangeness among some humans. So what exactly are we talking about? Beyond the vortexes, crystals, and magic, the weirdness was centered on the belief that the end of the Mayan calendar would produce such catastrophes that the world would come to an abrupt end. Just as in 1999, when people in Vilcabamba built bunkers and hunkered down to ride out the worldwide destruction of humanity, people spruced up their old bunkers or built new ones to ride out the date 12-21-2012.

Besides the renovated bunkers in Vilcabamba, a new set of bunkers was built just north of Paute, Ecuador, by a whole new set of survivalists and other nut cases. These people thought that their bunkers, at an altitude of about 7,500 ft., might survive the worldwide floods that were supposed to occur on the day of the end of the Mayan calendar. I guess they thought that parts of Ecuador would be spared from the total destruction of the rest of the world. Perhaps people were building bunkers in the Himalayas as well. There appears to be no appreciation of the force of gravity, which keeps seas at, well, sea level. If water from the oceans start flooding the Andes or the Himalayas at 7,500 ft. and higher, it means that Earth has left its orbit around the sun. Your bunker and all the provisions you stored in your bunker would be the least of your very short-term problems.

What did the true believers really think when they awakened New Year's Day 2000, or December 22, 2012, and everything was pretty much as it was the morning before? Evidence suggests that these people feel no shame as they begin preparing for the next great catastrophic threat to all of humankind.

Apparently, none of these people has picked up on the real threat of CO_2, ocean acidification, global climate change, and the myriad other problems, issues, and threats that really face humanity. After all, why let facts get in the way of a real bunker party?

My first encounter with true survivalists was about five years ago. We did not know they were true survivalists until after the encounter, but I will refer to them as survivalists throughout this narrative. My profession as a medical school professor and cancer research scientist pretty much spared me to some degree from encounters with these types of survivalists. It seems that there are few survivalist professors who believe in conspiracy theories. Now that I am retired and living in Ecuador with expats from California, Sedona, and yes, even Chicago, I am no longer spared.

The aftermath of this first encounter was entirely my fault. Estée and I met the survivalists in a Catholic church where God spared me from the fate of a lightning bolt, which I am sure He was considering. We were there to celebrate the Quinceañera of Betsey, the daughter of our friends, Pepe and Ingrid. Estée and I had been named the Padrinos to Betsey, which is something like god-parents. We were put in charge of providing spiritual guidance and advice to Betsey. God help her.

The survivalists had been invited as well. We will call them Pearl Silverbottom and Cash Goldfinger. They were married, but Pearl liked her silver bottom—sorry, her last name, Silverbottom—so she kept it. They were coming to Ecuador from a small town in southern Oregon to live as retirees like us. Pepe thought we had a lot in common and wanted us to meet. At first it seemed as if we did indeed have a lot in common. Ms. Silverbottom and Mr. Goldfinger seemed like pleasant people. After two weeks, they left to go back to their home in Oregon; we exchanged email addresses and began to communicate. This had been their first trip to Ecuador and they were hell-bent on finding land. I thought we could help them with lists of things to bring and things not to bring. I thought we could provide them with tales of our experiences that might help them in their move.

During one of the email exchanges, I was told that they were coming with a forty-foot container and they would stay in Ecuador permanently. Could I recommend a rental place until they got their container in two weeks max, probably less? Without consulting Estée, I e-blurted out an invitation to stay with us. It was going to be a maximum of two weeks, probably less. What could go wrong? The key phrases here are "without consulting" and "two weeks, max, probably less." Of course, "What could go wrong?" is another key phrase, but I don't want to overuse it. The invitation was rapidly accepted, and so two weeks, probably less, of houseguests had been arranged.

Estée took the news quite well, considering the lack of consultation. I would not have done so well. But how bad could it be? We began to find out how bad it could be when we got news that they were bringing three cats. I am sure our Doberman overheard this because he began to watch out the window and drool. These are usually not good signs in a Doberman. After a few months and many emails with lists and advice, all of which were entirely ignored, Ms. Silverbottom and Mr. Goldfinger showed up at the airport in Cuenca. I picked them up and we squeezed everything, including the three cats, into the Ford Explorer.

The first days went quite well. We kept the cats and the drooling Doberman separate. Estée cooked all the meals, our housekeeper cleaned all the rooms, and our houseguests generally enjoyed three-star, maybe higher, accommodations with little to no lifting of a silver bottom or a gold finger. Little glitches were handled, like the duct-taped cardboard on the guestroom window to hold out the little beam of light so Cash Goldfinger could sleep at night, and the adjustment to the shower of the guestroom so Cash had the proper amount of water pressure at the desired temperature. I sympathized because sleeping and showering are important to me too. In between the prepared meals and the room cleaning, our guests spent a lot of their time getting things done to prepare for their life in Ecuador.

After a few days, things began to fall apart. Pearl tried to help with the cooking and the cleanup after meals. After breaking several dishes of a set that is no longer produced, after slamming doors and drawers and chairs on floors, it was tactfully suggested that Pearl should refrain from trying to help. That is what she did with, in retrospect, an ever-so-slight smile at the corner of her mouth.

Then the real bad news came. Their container was delayed. It was stuck in Guayaquil and would not make it to Cuenca where it was supposed to go through customs. The container was in excess of five thousand pounds over-weight. The moving company in Oregon did not weigh the container; they estimated the weight. How does a moving company estimate the weight of a container? Do they get their employees to pick it up and kind of toss it in the air, then give a guess as to the weight? That exercise might be great entertainment at the local circus, but guessing the weight of a container in transit to Ecuador does not seem very professional.

The red flag went up for Ecuadorian customs officials, and there was nothing that could be done. The contents of the container were to be inspected in Guayaquil to see if Pearl and or Cash had added five thousand pounds of cigarettes or stinger missiles to their shipment. All the concerns of the unfolding events were vented over dinner each evening, served promptly at 6 p.m. to accommodate Cash's digestive issues, which were manifested in a series of spectacular, and unrestrained, burps and belches at all hours of the day. Estée has a reputation as a good cook. Pearl and Cash never missed breakfast, most lunches, and never, ever, a dinner.

Over dinner one evening, Pearl and Cash confided in us some of their concerns over having the contents of their container inspected. It turned out that Pearl and Cash had hidden away a number of things including, but not limited to, rare coins, gold, and silver—things that were on the "do not bring into Ecuador" list. There were other things that were only hinted at but not confirmed. There was an allusion to the need for firearms and ammunition. This information was just a hint, somewhat like the hint of the undetected weapons of mass destruction in Iraq.

Cash told me that guns were necessary because, in Oregon, they lived between two large cities, and when the unemployment rate in the United States moves to sixty to seventy percent any day now, and the stock market goes from seventeen thousand to seventeen, there will be food wars. The Silverbottoms and the Goldfingers of the world will be wiped off the face of the Earth in the tidal wave of hungry humanity looking for Pearl and Cash's refrigerator and their cupboard of canned goods. Cash told me that he had training from a special forces soldier. I was impressed. Cash, at a pudgy sixty-nine years old, did not look like the special forces type of guy. The training, it turned out, was a brief conversation with someone claiming to be a special forces soldier, who told Cash over the last of a twelve pack of beer that, "When they start shooting, keep moving. If you stop, they will get you."

The small bit of arugula that was on my salad fork heading toward my wide-open mouth never made it there. It fell off into my lap. My wide-open mouth stayed wide open. It took what seemed like minutes to digest the contents of the confession of gold, silver, and perhaps arms contraband, and the statement that "they" will get you. I finally asked the obvious, "Who are they?"

Cash's reply caused even more confusion in my mind: "You know, them, the ones that are after us."

There is a disease called paranoid schizophrenia, and it can be controlled to some degree by medication. Cash was not taking his medication. I quietly asked Pearl if she believed that "they" or "them" were after her as well. She thought "they" or "them" were. Pearl was not taking her medication either. It was clear that the pharmaceutical companies of the world needed to ramp up the production of anti-psychotic medication just for the expats in Ecuador.

The next day, after my restless night of dreaming of "they" and "them" and the need to keep moving, Pearl and Cash were off to look for a rental place. After several hours, Pearl burst into our house in tears, copious tears. "This is a third-world country!" she blurted out as her Max Factor eyeliner and mascara dribbled unevenly down her cheeks. "Everyone is poor!" she screamed, her voice getting more hysterical. "There are pigs everywhere! Everything is substandard! This is just not working for me! This is the worst mistake we have ever made in our lives!" She stormed down to her pig-free, not-so-poor, three-star-plus guestroom, slammed the door, and flopped onto the soft, comfortable mattress, sobbing.

Cash, who adores Pearl, tried to exert a calming influence. "She is a little stressed," he offered.

Promptly at 6 p.m., Pearl had recovered enough to pour herself a large glass of wine and be seated for dinner. Over Estée's famous flourless chocolate cake, I turned to Cash and asked, "Why did you come to Ecuador? What research did you do to prepare for your retirement?"

The answer was shocking to me but somewhat consistent with my other recent shocks. "I read about Ecuador in an article about retiring," he said.

I thought I heard correctly, but I had to ask. "An article, as in one article?" I questioned. "Not many articles and a lot of time to think this over?"

He affirmed that, indeed, he had read one article, not many articles. He did absolutely no research beyond the one article. He spent minutes, not even hours, thinking this through. Against our advice, they did not make multiple trips to get a "feel" for the country and its people. They did not look into the various possibilities of renting, buying, and/or building. They did nothing! They came once and purchased land, and then the second time to Ecuador was their move. I now began to understand. Actually, I thought I now began to understand, but there was more—oh, so much more—to come.

A part of me began to feel sorry for Pearl and Cash. It was a very small part of me, I must admit. We took them to the Gualaceo market on a sunny Tuesday afternoon. The official market days are Tuesday, Friday, and Sunday, but there are vendors there all week. The market is a two-square-block area that produces a sea of color, sounds, and smells that touch, or sometimes slap, your senses individually, or all at once. There are kids and stray dogs every-where, so you have to watch your step to avoid both. While you are looking down toward your steps in the outdoor part of the market, you are more than likely to hit your head on one of the brightly colored makeshift umbrellas that protect sellers and buyers alike from intermittent brief showers and bright sun. This is the vegetable and fruit market. Dead meat, fish, and poultry are to be found a few blocks away in another market. If your sense of hearing were good enough, which the human sense of hearing is not, you would know the direction of the meat market by the buzzing of the flies. Livestock is bartered in yet another market.

The four of us wandered up and down the narrow lanes between the dozens of sellers at the vegetable and fruit market when we happened upon another gringa. Estée and I do not want to become part of an expat community, so we generally do not initiate contact with gringos at the market, but Pearl struck up a conversation. The gringa—let's call her Gina—led us to her husband, Frank. Within thirty seconds, it was clear that Pearl and Cash had met their soul mates. Frank and Gina had moved to Gualaceo to grow food so when "they" and "them" come to get all of us, they could survive by growing food; never mind that they had left the food basket of the world in the Midwestern United States. I was waiting for the admonition that we should all keep moving when "they" come to get us.

A cold, clammy sweat came over me. These people were the second gringo couple to move to Gualaceo after us, and now Pearl and Cash would be the third couple. It was four against two, and who knew how many more would come. Gina and Frank wanted our phone number. I am ashamed to admit that I gave them a false number. Okay, not that ashamed. We have not seen them since.

It was 6 p.m., so it had to be dinnertime once again. We had a typical great meal because of Estée's effort, and we were lingering over dessert. Pearl was lingering over her fourth not-so-small glass of wine. More frequently now, it was getting harder and harder to come up with topics for dinner conversation. Estée is a good conversationalist and introduced the topic of newly found ways to inexpensively sterilize water, which could greatly help people in countries like those in Africa where water quality is an issue. Her conversation topic came from a short blurb in a *National Geographic* magazine.

Cash cleared his throat and said with true conviction, "That's not good. That would be like providing agar to bacteria. If you provide these human populations with clean water and, God help us, more food, they will simply breed like bacteria."

It was Estée's turn to drop her dessert. (We tried to take turns dropping things.) When you do not anticipate comments like this, and I don't see how it is possible to anticipate this comment, it is hard to quickly formulate a comeback. Usually, the comeback is, at first, sputtering gibberish. I was at a loss for words. Estée's quick if not very well-thought-out comeback was akin to an attack by a stealth fighter with a smart bomb. "You sound worse than the Nazis," was her comment.

Pearl took immediate umbrage and noted that her great grandmother on her father's side was part Jewish, or so she thought. We all looked at each other and tried to decide how that fit into anything, let alone the conversation. The confused pause was perfect because it prevented us from coming to further verbal blows.

By now, I had time to ponder the gist of Cash's comment. "But Cash," I ventured, "wouldn't your argument mean that countries like Denmark, Germany, Switzerland, Holland, even the United States—countries with the most 'agar'— would have the highest birth rates? In fact, they have the lowest birth rates."

Nothing more was said on the subject that evening, or on any other evening. By now, we were into our third week of what was supposed to be two weeks max, probably less. I went to bed in a piss-poor mood.

To me, memory is an incredible and mysterious set of chemical events that your brain engages in without too much prompting by you. I have an intense curiosity about what memory really is and how it works. Many years ago, I was privileged to introduce Dr. Eric Kandel at a meeting at Rush-Presbyterian St. Luke's Medical Center. I was appointed scientific chairman of the sesquicentennial celebration at Rush, and as such, I got to introduce some of the notable speakers. He would not remember me, of course, but I certainly remember him.

Dr. Kandel outlined studies he and his colleagues had done on neural tracks in the sea snail, *Aplysis californica,* and found that as memory increased through training, new proteins were produced along neural tracks and nearby synapses. It turned out from a large number of studies in the snail and other more complex systems that this process was linked to memory. Dr. Kandel was awarded the Nobel Prize in 2000. It should have been awarded to him much earlier, but it was fitting that the year 2000 was selected, a year that is easy to remember.

It was exactly 7:12 p.m. on a Tuesday evening that my brain sprung into action and produced so much memory protein that I will never forget the moment. At that moment on that Tuesday evening, Cash leaned slightly forward, looked me in the eyes, and in the conversational lull that was more and more frequent into the third week of the Silverbottom/Goldfinger stay, said, "You know that the U.S. military flew those planes into the New York Trade Towers on 9/11."

I emitted a little chuckle and looked at the chicken bones on my plate to see if there was something I could feed our Doberman, since he had been denied any taste of the three cats. I looked up to see that Cash was deadly serious. I often say, "you're kidding" in these kinds of situations for lack of anything intelligent to say. This time, I said, "You're cashing me in, aren't you Cash?" The poor pun was ignored. If I am at an appropriate place, I simply get up and walk away, not wanting to spend another second with such stupid fools. After I said, "you're cashing me in," I resisted the very strong urge to leave, mostly because this was my house and I really did not have anywhere to go. Cash assured me that, no, he was not joking. All the news of the terrorist attacks was a ruse, and the United States government was hiding all the information. It was a grand conspiracy.

I try to refrain from profanity, since I think it is undignified, but "no shit" came out without thinking. Cash informed me that this was common knowledge.

"Common to whom?" I asked.

"Everyone," was his reply. I was so shocked that I did not know how to respond, but it was clear that Cash did not consider me part of everyone. I felt the blood rise to my head. I physically became tense, combative, and ready for a fight, but how can one fight against such a totally absurd assertion?

"So all those people who died in the planes that flew into the Trade Towers, the Pentagon, or into the ground in Pennsylvania were actually not dead, they were really not there, right?"

"That's correct," replied Cash. "And how about all the people in the Trade Towers and the Pentagon? Are they dead?"

"Oh yes, they were all killed by our own government," Cash said very seriously.

I know people who make up stuff just to get a reaction. I don't appreciate these people and I avoid them, but there are those who do it. I was now trying to get a sense if Cash was such a person. I didn't want to rise to the bait, if indeed, it was bait, until I knew if Cash was being serious. The "they" and "them" discussion made me believe that he was serious. He went on to describe how the United States government flew drone planes into the buildings. They were unmanned drones.

"Why?" seemed like a silly question at this point, but what the hell, let's go all the way.

"So we could invade Iraq and take all the oil," was the quick answer.

I was starting to get into this, so I asked, "Then why are we paying full market price for Iraq's oil?"

Cash sensed hostility and not just a little of it.

"No, really, it just does not make any sense," I said with hostility brimming over. I turned to Pearl and asked her if she believed this crap as well. I suppose the use of the phrase "this crap" may have prejudiced the answer. She looked a little sheepish but admitted that, yes, she was on board with these ideas as well.

Every fiber in my body wanted to get up from the table and ask them to pack their bags and leave. Estée had to usher me into the bedroom where we had the "we have to make guests feel welcome" conversation. The intruders stayed on. Now we were into our fourth week with no end in sight.

It was six o'clock in the evening and therefore, it was dinnertime yet again. On this particular evening the conversation centered on the Gulf oil spill. I just couldn't wait for this one. Cash did not disappoint. "You know that British Petroleum could have stopped the flow of oil any time," he started.

"Oh, really, then why didn't they?" I asked warily.

"Because they didn't want to. Look, they retrieved about sixty percent of the flow, so they were doing fine. Besides, there is a leak five miles away that is spewing twice the amount of oil into the Gulf than the Deep Water Horizon did. The U.S. government is covering it up."

I began to smirk. "How do you know that?" I said in a bemused tone.

Cash said, and I am not making this up, "A Russian submarine reported it."

"Oh," I replied, "so it is on the news."

"Well, not on CNN or BBC or any of those left-wing broadcasts," said Cash.

"How about Fox News, the fair and unbiased right-wing broadcast station?" I asked, giving away a little of my own bias.

"No, it is on the Internet," said Cash.

I later searched the Internet and found absolutely nothing. Cash was always going to give me the link to the sensational story, but never got around to it. It is strange how the amount of new oil in the Gulf went down when the flow from the Deep Water Horizon was shut off. What happened to the horrific oil spill five miles away? Perhaps, in an act of sacrificial bravery, the Russian submarine dove into the gaping oil gushing hole and plugged it up for the sake of all humanity. Something like the story of the little Dutch boy who put his finger in the dyke in The Netherlands and saved the town from flooding. I liked my story. It was definitely better than the crap Cash was putting out there.

Into the fifth week of Pearl and Cash's stay, their container finally showed up in Cuenca. By now, they had secured a rental apartment in Cuenca, thank God, and not in Gualaceo. They signed a two-year contract to rent a nice apartment. Estée, Nora, and I had plans to go to Peru to start the recovery process of five weeks of craziness. On Thursday, we described our plans to leave on the following Monday. Pearl and Cash's expressions were blank. They wished us a good time. I finally had to tell Cash, not without some inner satisfaction, that we did not want anyone except our employees and our Doberman staying in our house while we were gone. He seemed surprised. "I don't see how we can move into our rental. We do not have a refrigerator yet in the rental house to store cool milk for my coffee," was his response.

"GET THE F*#K OUT OF MY HOUSE…NOW!" was my response. Under these circumstances, Catholic priests would use foul language, but they have the advantage of being able to confess. I can't, but then, I have never felt the urge to confess.

In some respects, I have never recovered. I have never had the displeasure to meet people like this before, and I never want to again. Pearl said one evening toward the end of the fourth week over her fifth glass of wine (it easily could have been the fifth week over her fourth glass of wine), "I guess we are not like many other people, are we?" "No," Cash replied with great pride, "we certainly are not."

My mother had a clever saying that I stole for my own. She used to say after some silly conversations about government conspiracies, vortexes, or crystals—views and opinions that she scorned—"Everyone in the whole world is crazy, except you and me—and sometimes I am really worried about you!" I did not know it for so many years, shielded as I was by an academic life, but there really are crazy people out there, a lot of them. It seems like most of them have or are in the process of moving to Ecuador. This makes me sad.

Another example of people who we wish were not in Ecuador, or at least people we wish we never met, are "Penelope Pennywise" and "Freddy Hornblower." Freddy is a distant relative of Horatio. They are a little less crazy than Pearl Silverbottom and Cash Goldfinger, but just as litigious, thus the ever-so-slight alterations in their names. We met Penelope and Freddy through a mutual friend. They have honed the art of thoroughly taking advantage of everyone around them, and even the friends of everyone around them.

We would invite Penelope and Freddy to our home quite often because at first, they seemed like pleasant people. If you are going to take advantage of everyone around you, you really need to be pleasant. After many Estée-prepared lunches, which would sometimes stretch into Estée-prepared dinners, which could stretch into wine-sipping/guzzling evenings by the fireplace, Estée noticed that she was doing all the cooking, the cleanup, and the wine opening. We never got invited to Penelope and Freddy's house for lunch, dinner, or wine. This was turning into a one-way street of entertainment. Penelope told us that their stove was broken and they were getting a new one. As soon as the new stove was installed, we would be invited to the inaugural meal and many meals after that to make up for the obvious one-way street of entertainment. Even they recognized the one-way sign. It never happened. Since we had a number of mutual acquaintances, the four of us would be invited to lunches given by these kind Ecuadorians. On the occasion of one such lunch, Freddy, in a whispered aside, said, "You know, if we play our cards right, we might get invited to enough lunches so that we won't have to buy many groceries, and we will rarely have to cook." I began to get the picture. Their real names were Penelope and Freddy Freeloader.

It got worse. Our friends Carlos and Marti along with Dave and Bev arrived for a visit, and we went out to eat at Corvel, one of our favorite restaurants in Paute. We walked in to find Penelope and Freddy just about to order. They invited us to join them and out of politeness, we sat down at the same table. When it was time to pay the bill, Penelope and Freddy, in a synchronized movement worthy of a sophisticated professional dance move, gracefully sashayed off to separate toilets. Carlos, Dave and I paid the bill, the whole bill. Five minutes later and, I'm sure, after many hand washings, they emerged still synchronized to thank us profusely for dinner. The Freeloaders struck again.

Since our experiences with Pearl Pennywise and her husband, Cash Hornblower, along with Penelope Silverbottom and her husband, Freddy Goldfinger (perhaps I am getting a little confused at this point), we have met some great expats in Ecuador. I am happy that I can use their names undisguised, names like Jason, Donna, Edward, Paul, Karen, Diane and many more, and we are confident that they will become friends on some level. My confidence and my faith in humanity are slowly being restored—very slowly. We still see the Freeloaders once in a while at lunches. They still have a few cards that they play well.

It has been years now since we have seen Pearl and Cash. We learned that after a few months, they moved from their rental apartment in the middle of the night. The landlord is looking for them to pay their two-year legal contract. I am not surprised because that is the kind of people they are. I am sure it was some sort of conspiracy from the beginning. Very thankfully, they moved west, not east toward us. I doubt we will ever see them again. I don't know how I would react if I did see them, but if it happens, I think I will keep moving, just in case the Silverbottoms and the Goldfingers are the "they" and "them." Keep moving! And if you hear shots ring out, remember, serpentine, serpentine!

chapter 11

Trouble in Paradise:
The Great El Pangui Shoot-Out and Oh So Much More

El Pangui is a small, lazy town located in southeast Ecuador on the east slopes of the Andes at an elevation of eight hundred meters. It is in an area called The Oriente in the Province of Zamora. It is sustained mainly by agriculture, fiestas, and alcoholic beverages (in reverse order). The streets of El Pangui are laid out like nearly all Ecuadorian villages, with a main street and a Catholic church whose front doors open onto a street that surrounds a town square. These squares or parks are usually festooned with an array of beautiful plants and flowers that vary with the altitude of the park and the microclimate of the area. El Pangui, which means "boa constrictor" in the Shuar language, is inhabited mostly by the Shuar or descendants of the Shuar Indians. And then there is Chuck.

Chuck is a tall, thin, disheveled, white-haired, grisly bearded, seventy-nine-year-old gringo curmudgeon who is angry eighty percent of the time and a kindly, wise gentleman twenty percent of the time with absolutely nothing in between. Actually, it is closer to eighty-five and fifteen percent, but I won't quibble. Chuck is a world-class expert on a type of plant called a succulent. He knows a great deal about plants in general and is shocked by those ignorant masses who do not know about, or are not interested in, succulents or plants in general. He uses the phrase "you don't know that?" often and incredulously. That phrase tends to dispel any warm and fuzzy feeling that one might have toward Chuck, but I doubt that matters to him.

123

Chuck and his kind, sweet wife Karen retired from the secluded hinterlands near Council Bluffs, Iowa, to the secluded hinterlands west of the town of El Pangui. Karen is a cardiologist and was in the process of joining Chuck permanently—we thought. She announced a delay in her visit to El Pangui, and Estée and I mused that she may have changed her mind about either living in El Pangui, living with Chuck, or both. However, her delay was because of a detached retina, which healed over a short time, and she did come back. They enjoy the seclusion, and while it is not for everyone, the landscape is beautiful in many respects; plants grow quickly and the snakes are plentiful. Never mind the fact that we have never seen one. We know they are lurking everywhere.

Estée and I met Chuck and Karen several years ago in Ecuador; however, Estée's aversion to and my healthy respect for the unseen snakes preclude our spending a lot of time in a town called Boa Constrictor.

Estée and I received a call from an excited Chuck at about nine on a July morning. He incredulously proclaimed, "They're shooting; they're really shooting!!" Immediately I thought of Pearl and Cash and thought, "My god, it has started." "They" or "them" are after Chuck and his food. I had no idea that "they" or "them" were so widespread throughout the land that "they" or "them" could possibly be in El Pangui. "Keep moving," came to mind, along with "serpentine, serpentine!"

He proceeded to inform us that there were police and military vehicles and personnel lined up on the road immediately west of his property. They were shooting at a small, shack-like house in the center of a thirty-hectare plot of land used as a pasture for a herd of cows. The police and military personnel were decked out in their finest camouflage outfits—never mind that compared to the colors they were surrounded by, they stuck out like police and military personnel with the wrong camouflage. Whoever was in the shack was shooting back.

There were a few trees scattered throughout the land where cows normally grazed peacefully, but since the land was fairly flat, there were few things except the cows to stop bullets from either direction. Not knowing where the cows were at the moment, I thought that there might be some beef brisket along with short ribs coming on the market in short order. The shooting from the authorities emanated from high-powered automatic rifles. Grenade launchers were in evidence as well. Missing were tanks, Apache attack helicopters, and F-16 fighter planes. It is very unlikely that World War III would start in El Pangui, Ecuador, but one could not argue against that possibility on that particular July morning. There were approximately fifty heavily armed and seriously, if incorrectly, camouflaged men shooting at one small shack.

The disconcerting thing was that whoever was in the shack was shooting back with what proved to be high-powered rifles as well. The even more disconcerting thing, at least for Chuck, was that the authorities were crouching behind their military vehicles right in front of his newly constructed house. Chuck was the only human in the house; however, there were seven Dachshunds who were thrilled by the activity. While Chuck had to crouch and run in a serpentine path to avoid the windows, the Dachshunds had the advantage of being able to stand as tall as their five-inch legs would allow and still be quite safe—just one of many advantages of being a Dachshund.

The battle started at 8:47 a.m. and proceeded off and on during the morning until exactly 1 p.m. The authorities then rose in unison, got into their wrongly camouflaged vehicles, and drove off. It was lunchtime. Promptly at 3 p.m., the vehicles reentered the road in a cloud of dust. The authorities got out of their vehicles, crouched down behind them, and commenced firing with their automatic rifles. We assume that the human targets in the shack had lunch at a different restaurant in El Pangui than the authorities did; however, that is not necessarily a given. If they chose the same restaurant, I'm sure they sat at different tables.

During lunch break, Chuck had a chance to reconnoiter the west side of his property and, to his horror, he found a crushed bullet on the sidewalk surrounding his house. There was a mark in the brick above the crushed bullet, making it obvious that a stray or not-so-stray shot had found the house. Chuck stayed low the rest of the day and the Dachshunds stayed even lower without trying. At exactly 6 p.m., close to sundown, the authorities packed up and drove off in a cloud of dust. Whatever was happening appeared to be over, at least for the day, but what was going on? Who was in the shack that the authorities were so intent on shooting?

Chuck called our mutual friend, Pepe, who happened to have grown up in El Pangui and who knew most of the people and the activities that made up daily life there. Pepe called his brother, Luis, the mayor of El Pangui, and got the scoop. Remember, this is a very small town, and like every small town the world over, everyone knows the scoop. It turns out that a very unscrupulous non-Shuar person (anyone who isn't a Shuar is simply a non-Shuar) cheated a Shuar couple out of the thirty hectares of land and the small shack that resides in the middle of the property. He did this unscrupulous thing sixteen years ago by paying a lawyer to draw up false papers simply saying that the unscrupulous non-Shuar person owned the thirty hectares and the shack. At first blush, one could say that this is impossible; however, Estée and I know that it is not impossible.

Our wonderful and friendly neighbor across the San Francisco River from us tried to do the exact same thing. Thankfully, we were not the targets, but we discovered that our neighbor had false papers drawn up and notarized, showing that she owned the land adjacent to her, which contained a quite-large house on two hectares of very beautiful land. Near us, land is going for a minimum of $30 per square meter, so we are talking about $600,000 just for the five acres of land. While that may be pocket change in downtown New York or London, that is not pocket change in Ecuador. That is grand theft in any country and in any language, no matter how notarized the papers may be.

In El Pangui, land is not quite as expensive, but thirty hectares is still worth a lot of change. The Shuar couple who legally owned the land passed away, one after the other. They had twelve children and the children knew that their parents had been cheated out of the land. They wanted it back. So, at least part of the puzzle was solved. Some of the twelve children of the legal owners of the land and the shack were holed up and shooting at the authorities.

Now one would think that the large number of lawyers in the world, and the extraordinarily large number of lawyers in Ecuador, might be justified by this one case. This is a chance for not-very-clever lawyers to bring the full weight of the law crushing down on that unscrupulous non-Shuar person. Great pride would be felt around the conference tables of law firms as the land and the shack were restored to the rightful owners. It could easily be proven that the papers that the non-Shuar person presented to the authorities were false. Case closed. The case would be taught in law classes in Ecuador and perhaps throughout Latin America, if not in other countries where the oppressed can have their land stolen by false papers. John Grisham could write law novels based on this case. Everyone could be made happy by the obvious outcome of the very public trial in the courthouse in Loja with great cheers for the downtrodden.

Sadly, this was not the way it unfolded. I was told that while the indigenous Quechua Indians that live in the high Sierras, including our town of Gualaceo, thrive and are thrilled by employing lawyers to cheat others out of land and to protect themselves from being cheated out of land, the Shuar Indians solve their problems in different ways. In this case, the solution was taking back their land by force. My rather naive question was: "If the land was illegally obtained by the non-Shuar person, who gave the police and the military the authority to force the rightful owners to give up the land?" That seemed like a reasonable and appropriate question. Was it the mayor, Louis, Pepe's brother? I really hoped it was not. Silly me, it was the non-Shuar person himself. He simply showed the false papers to a police commander, and with the help of some military personnel who needed to dust off some of their unused arsenal, the shooting began.

Day two started peacefully. The Dachshunds barked Chuck awake at their usual 6 a.m. and Chuck let them bolt out of their crates into a whole new day. Chuck dressed in his usual pair of faded jeans that still had a little of the original blue color. In concert with the old jeans, he wore an old but favorite t-shirt stating, "Heaven is a State of Euphorbia" (a genus of succulent plant, the details of which Chuck is an expert..."You didn't know that?"). A pair of sandals worn without socks finished off the ensemble. Chuck made coffee and sat on the east side of the house overlooking the valley where El Pangui began to stir. The sky began to brighten, showing light layers and folds of blue-gray ground fog blending into higher layers of rose-colored clouds. The Cordillera del Cóndor began to take shape off in the distance toward Peru. The ground emitted a humid, earthy smell that reminded Chuck why the plants seemed to grow several inches each day. He had high hopes that the great El Pangui shootout was history—a minor page in the total history of El Pangui.

So there was some fear and much trepidation when Chuck saw a cloud of dust rising from the single road that came from El Pangui toward his land. The police and the military personnel lined up their bullet-pocked vehicles on the road next to Chuck's house and disembarked with their automatic weapons and grenade launchers.

There was one new twist. Chuck saw a small, single-engine spotter plane circling overhead—Ecuador's version of AWAX, in which a person leans out the window with a pair of binoculars and points. Under these circumstances, it is just as effective as AWAX. This would suggest that the target was either missing or it was at least obscured. This did not stop the shooting. The authorities opened fire, shooting in a variety of directions.

Chuck ducked; the Dachshunds stood tall and sounded the alarm with a ferocious symphony of barking, baying, hooting, and howling. This was getting serious. Someone might get hurt. Indeed, a high-powered rifle bullet did wound someone on the authority's side. An army vehicle carried him off to the regional hospital in Loja. Midday came and the authorities packed up as they had on the previous day. Chuck was fully expecting the war to commence promptly at 3 p.m. that afternoon, but no one returned. It appeared that the war was over. There was nothing on CNN International. Fox News missed it entirely, but if they had reported the incident, it would clearly have been the liberals' fault and part of a plot.

What was worse was that it was impossible to find out what the outcome was. Was Chuck going to be living in fear into the foreseeable future? Was he going to have an unscrupulous non-Shuar person living next door, or was he going to have Shuar neighbors with high-powered rifles who were quite willing to use them to settle land and probably other disputes?

The answer came several months later when construction started on six small houses with their front doors facing the road directly across from Chuck's house. The Shuars had won, and of all the possible locations on the thirty hectares to build, they had decided to be as close to Chuck as possible. So much for isolation.

Alcohol, fiestas, and agriculture are not the only activities and commodities in El Pangui. It is a territory rich in gold and copper. There is a large number of gold mines in the area, and the current government wants to build a very big open-pit copper mine complete with trucks running on tires two stories high or more. The government assured the Shuar that the copper mine would be eco-friendly. "We are the government; trust us." The Shuar did not.

So it was not a great surprise that, once again, we got a call from Chuck. We knew that he was supposed to be on his way from El Pangui through Chigüinda, through Sig Sig and Chordeleg (named after a three-legged cow, a bad joke) to Gualaceo. Chuck made it about six kilometers out of El Pangui before a road-block and a large group of people brought him to a screeching halt. Roadblocks in Ecuador usually consist of burning tires fed by brush and gasoline. The huge cloud of billowing black smoke told Chuck that this was the usual roadblock. The billowing black smoke was accompanied by a large group of people who were acting more like a mob of angry and partially to totally inebriated Shuar. Two men with shotguns rushed at Chuck's Toyota pickup, and one pointed his gun into the cabin. This got Chuck's attention. His attention was wasted to some degree since they were shouting words that Chuck did not understand, either in Shuar or in Spanish. I don't think it would have mattered if their shouting and yelling were in English or Turkish; if you have a gun at your head, your concen-tration is pretty much on the end of the gun barrel and what might come out of it. It is not that you could duck in time, or put your hand up to stop it, but the end of the barrel still presented a riveting focal point during the one-sided conversation.

Just when it appeared that things were about to get catastrophically worse, an older woman came up alongside the truck and, in a barely audible voice, spoke to the gentleman holding the gun pointed at Chuck's nose. "I don't think he works for the mine. I have seen him with the people from Ecuagenera, the orchid company. He is a friend of Pepe, the mayor's brother." The man with the gun smiled, withdrew his gun barrel from the end of Chuck's nose, said, "Have a good day" in Shuar, turned, and shuffled off to perhaps bag a real miner.

If I were Chuck, I would not bother to clean out my pants, let alone my underwear. I would just throw them away. Chuck went back home weaving, not from drink, but from an ensuing nervous tremor with occasional ticks that prevented him from driving straight. Sweat dribbled from his pores and he was more than just a little thrilled to walk back into his house among the Dachshunds. His voice was still cracking up when he was able to call to tell us the story and why he would not be coming to Gualaceo in the near future.

Chuck likes living in El Pangui and I like to visit. He and Karen built a beautiful house on thirteen acres of partially wooded land. They had a specific house plan in mind and had an architect plan a three-bedroom house with a kitchen, living room, and dining room combined under a vaulted ceiling with huge wood beams. The architect turned over the drawings to the contractor whom Pepe recommended, named Gordo, or "fat boy" in Spanish. The architect and Gordo had never seen a house design like this one. Gordo assured Chuck that building this house was well within his house-building capabilities. "What could go wrong? Don't worry about it!" were phrases that Gordo uttered frequently. We had shared our experience with these phrases with Chuck, so he began to sweat, not just during the night, but during the day as well.

The construction seemed to get off to a good start. Material was delivered, the foundation was poured, and walls began to take shape. The fact that the corners were not exactly ninety degrees was only a minor inconvenience, part of which meant that a row or two of tile would have to be custom cut to piece into the irregular space left by walls that were not parallel. Cabinets would be a little odd in their shape, but these things would have to be pointed out to be very noticeable. The house took on a very slight Picasso-esque quality, but only if framed in Picasso-esque narrative by the owner.

In the middle of construction, Gordo approached Chuck and asked for an additional $10,000. Gordo explained that he had not estimated a pitched roof, which produced a vaulted ceiling, but had figured the construction costs on a flat roof. Now, if you looked at the plans, the one feature that stuck out more than any other was the striking vaulted ceiling with the accompanying pitched roof. What part of that could Gordo miss? According to Gordo, he missed the whole thing. Chuck very reluctantly paid Gordo the extra $10,000. It was either that or find a new contractor, and no one wants to do that in the middle of a building project. With the infusion of new money, the project proceeded. The plumbing was put in place, the electrical work was completed, and the tile roof was laid into place on the newly paid for pitched roof. Chuck was ready to move in.

No more than a day went by when we got a call from Chuck. "I am sitting here with pots and pans catching the water from the leaks in the roof. That mangy bastard Gordo did not know what he was doing!" yelled Chuck. I am taking the liberty to clean up the language here since this is a story for the whole family. I could envision Chuck angrily running from pot to pan, emptying the fuller ones, and moving from spot to spot, finding new leaks almost every minute. The leaks were in the bedrooms, in the garage, and especially from the vaunted vaulted ceiling.

As the days went by and the number of leaks increased, Chuck sought out Gordo to make good on his construction project, the one that was well within his construction knowledge. Gordo was nowhere to be found. Pepe could not find him; Gordo's siblings could not find him; not even Gordo's parents could find him. Chuck was stuck and quite wet to boot. Thankfully, it quit raining for a few days, but we continued to hear from Chuck with new stories regarding questionable construction practices and their inevitable consequences. Every time Chuck turned on the light on the narrow veranda, the light would glow very brightly for a fraction of a second and then blow out. He replaced it and the blowout was repeated. Chuck had a voltage meter, which measured 220 volts in the 110-volt socket. It was just too much for the poor 110-volt light bulb.

Days went by, the leaky roof leaked whenever there was rain—which was often in El Pangui—and Gordo stayed missing. Finally, Chuck got someone to fix the leaks. A ladder was placed next to the roof, and the worker ascended to effect repairs. That effort did not last long. Within less than a minute, the worker was in the doorway with eyes very wide open. This turned out to be good news since the worker could have been dead.

The roof repairman tried as best he could to inform Chuck that the roof was electric. Chuck was fond of his roof notwithstanding the leaks, but to describe it as electric was of another generation than Chuck came from. Chuck thanked him and told him to please fix the leaks. The roofer persevered, and finally Chuck began to understand that the term "electric" was not a compliment, as in, "your roof is electrifying," but referred to the fact that the roof was truly electrified.

Chuck climbed up enough rungs to reach the roof and gingerly touched the tile. It was electrified. The whole roof very likely emitted a faint glow at night if the humidity was above a certain threshold. Once the electricity to the house was shut off, the roof no longer glowed. How could this be? Once the roof was dismantled to repair the leaks, it was found that a nail used to secure the flashing was pounded through the roof into an electric wire. Electricity poured through the nail into the metal flashing, and if the roof was wet, as it almost always was, the whole roof was "electric," which could provide a shocking experience. That problem, along with the multiple leaks, was sort of fixed. After two years, the total number of leaks was down to about four.

Chuck's wife, Karen, was in a transitional period of her life. She was younger than Chuck and wanted to make the passage into retirement slowly. Chuck was less patient, partly because he needed someone to help empty the water from the pots and pans sitting under the leaks. Karen came to Ecuador for several months at a time, so she was beginning to enjoy the tropical surroundings. One of Karen's passions is horseback riding. As a result, two horses were purchased to occupy part of the thirteen acres of land. Unfortunately, one of the horses died of unknown causes. Later, a mule was purchased to keep the remaining horse company.

One day, the phone rang and caller ID identified the caller as Chuck. "The gosh-darn mule (again cleaned-up language) escaped and took the horse with him." My first inclination was to ask if it was not the gosh-darn horse that escaped and took the mule with him, but with Chuck, it is better to just listen. As the story unfolded, we found out that Chuck's employee, Maria, had gotten on her motor scooter and began asking around if anyone had seen a dark brown horse and an almost-white mule walking together. Most people had not seen them, but others had, so Maria began to track the wayward horse and mule down. Maria was headed in what she was sure was the right direction. She kept asking if people had seen a dark brown horse and an almost-white mule walking together, but now the reply was negative. However, people had seen a dark brown horse and three mules, one of which was almost white, walking toward a town called Gualaquiza. This was seriously funny, but one dare not show mirth to an angry Chuck. Estée, who had taken the call, kept her mirth well hidden, but when she hung up, there were some loud guffaws. The only thing that could have added to the scene was the addition of some dogs and a cat, perhaps with a mouse on its back, all going on their great adventure to Gualaquiza.

In January, the phone rang, and as usual, I glanced at the caller ID to discover another call from Chuck. After a few pleasantries, Chuck asked if I was sitting down. I told him no, but I could be if necessary. I was hoping that Chuck's health was not an issue. It was not. Karen, who had been back in El Pangui for about two months, awoke one morning to discover that she was not ready to retire.

The whole issue of when someone is ready to retire is a very complex one and probably different for each individual. For many people, the biggest resistance to retirement is the fear that you will wake up one morning and discover that you really were not ready to retire. Some people may never be ready to retire; they will simply not wake up one morning. Karen did wake up, and she announced to Chuck that she needed to be needed by cardiac patients back in the U.S.—not just in the U.S., but in Nebraska, near the area where they previously lived.

Chuck, after lecturing Estée and me on how excruciating the winters were in the Midwest (as if we didn't know), was now moving back to the Midwest. Chuck and I ruminated for a few minutes on the high cost of loving women, and then I hung up to tell Estée the news and to tell her I loved her. Part of me was genuinely sad. Beyond the entertainment value, I had gotten to like Chuck to the degree that anyone could like Chuck, or more properly stated, to the degree that Chuck would allow anyone to like him. Karen was more likable—okay, a lot more likeable—and I was sad to see them leave. After all, how was I going to learn about succulent plants? This was not going to be a trivial relocation. Just moving the Dachshunds, which now numbered ten, was going to be a challenge.

No wonder Chuck is angry eighty percent of the time—okay, it is more like eighty-five percent of the time. His house has been shot at. He was threatened with a gun. He has multiple leaks in his electrified roof and Gordo is nowhere to be found. The almost-white mule is an escape artist that makes Chuck think that the previous owner unloaded it on Chuck to get rid of it. But, according to Chuck, El Pangui is paradise, and an unscrupulous non-Shuar person has yet to try to take his land. And now to top it all off, Chuck was going to be boiled in the summer and buried in snow during the winter while subjected to some serious cold weather. I hope he saved his long johns. Long live Chuck.

chapter 12

Education in Ecuador:
A Short Venture into the Unknown

As I slowly opened the envelope that came in the mail to the house in Oak Park earlier that day in April 2006, anxiety crept into my mind. The return address on the envelope said "Cook County Assessor," and in bold letters on the envelope, it said, "IMPORTANT, YOUR SIX MONTH ESTIMATED PROPERTY TAXES ARE ENCLOSED. DO NOT DISCARD." In Oak Park, that was enough to bring a small-to-large bead of sweat to the brow and a slight-to-knee-bending feeling of anxiety. In situations such as these, it does not matter if the envelope is slowly torn open to gently reveal the content or if it is ripped open to flood the senses with what has been, since 1984, a rapidly increasing shock of a tax bill.

Property taxes are supposed to be linked to the value of the property. As the bubble of property values increased through the late 1980s, throughout the 1990s, and past the supposed end of the world in 2000 and beyond, it was expected that property taxes would go up, although in Oak Park, the upward slope of the exponential curve was extraordinary. When the housing bubble burst, the increase in property taxes in Oak Park did not skip a beat. There was absolutely no glitch in the upward trend, not even a hint that your precious house was now priced more like an outhouse. The bill I was holding in my hand was in the amount of $6,824.71. That was for half the year, and I would get the final bill for the year in September or October, which would be higher still. The total would be close to $14,000 with the promise of a higher total the next year.

With shaky legs, I walked outdoors to the patio table and sat down to go line by line through the itemized list of things for which I was paying $6,824.71.

As I reviewed the list of items, a large mosquito landed on my arm and settled in for a meal of my fairly rare AB+ blood. I noticed that one of the items near the bottom of the list was a fee of $4.21 for mosquito abatement. Just before I swatted the mosquito and brushed the remains off my arm, I swear she looked up at me and I saw the face of the Cook County assessor sucking my blood.

Then I got to the two biggest items: $2,170.26 for Mann Elementary School and $2,006.46 for Oak Park-River Forest High School. In Oak Park, as in many communities throughout the United States, we place a high value on education—never mind the fact that in many communities, the quality of that education is suspect. Although not universal, one can rightly assume that in communities with high property values, and therefore high property taxes, schools are better because they have adequate resources. Since money for public schools comes from property taxes, poorer communities have fewer resources, creating a perpetual schism between the haves and the have-nots. This is a political issue, one that does not seem to be high on any politician's list of things to solve.

One of the first questions prospective buyers ask when considering moving into a community is the ranking of the public school compared to other schools. These rankings are on the Internet, and usually buyers with children are very aware of the rankings when looking for a home. Churches come second unless they have an attached school. There are many Catholic families living in North Oak Park expressly to send their kids to St. Giles, at a cost of several thousand dollars a semester. They pay this Catholic tuition in addition to property taxes. If you have multiple children, which many Catholic parents do, you had better have a substantial inheritance, a large income, or better, both. Sherry, my daughter, went to a Montessori school until she was twelve years old at a not-so-trivial cost. None of these costs was covered in my property tax bill, nor would I expect them to be covered. The largest increase in the tax bill from year to year was for the schools.

In the end, all my neighbors agreed at the annual block party that the quality of the schools increases the overall desirability of the community, thereby increasing the property values—that is, until the bubble burst. When property values dropped like Galileo's iron balls from the Tower of Pisa, property taxes should have dropped as well, right? If they had, the schools would be getting less, which may decrease the quality, and thus the desirability, of Oak Park in general. Would this be the right thing to do? Probably not.

The mechanism that the Cook County Assessor's Office used to counter the dropping property values was to rapidly increase the assessment multiplier, as dictated by the governing body of the Village of Oak Park. The net result was that our property taxes did not fall, and while Galileo's balls continued to fall from the force of gravity, Oak Park's property taxes were firmly, if counterintuitively, suspended in air and actually going up. This is scientific proof that gravity, including the crushing gravity within black holes, does not have any effect on taxes.

That night, I presented the bill to Estée, not to pay but to be as amazed as I had been earlier that day. I certainly would have accepted the offer to pay from Estée, but none came. She looked through the items and nodded until she got to the $4.21 for mosquito abatement, the smallest amount on the bill; then she went ballistic. That spring had been an exceptionally nasty one considering the bloodletting from the massive number of mosquitoes, and Estée wanted to know exactly how they were being abated. The next day, she took the bill to work and, during a break, called the Village of Oak Park to discuss the issue of mosquito abatement. There was a faintly audible snicker from the receptionist as she forwarded Estée's call to someone who was supposed to know something about the abatement program.

Three forwarded people later, a rather confused man came on the line to say that the Village of Oak Park did not handle the mosquito abatement program. That program was handled by the Des Plains Park District. He had the phone number, and again, that snicker was faint but clearly audible. Estée is tenacious, so it was no surprise that she called the Des Plains Park District. Estée was put through to the assistant manager of the Des Plains Park District in charge of the mosquito abatement program. The conversation went like this:

Estée: "Sir, I live in Oak Park, and I was told by someone at the village office that you are responsible for the mosquito abatement program in Oak Park. Is that true?"

Assistant Manager: "The what program?"

Estée: "The mosquito abatement program."

Assistant Manager: "What is that? I don't know what you are talking about."

Estée: "Don't you spray for mosquitoes?"

Assistant Manager: "Oh, spraying for mosquitoes! Oh, no, we have not done that for years. Someone said that the chemicals in the spray were not safe, so we quit. Sometimes we put some anti-mosquito pellets in the sewers. "

Estée: "Do you do that in Oak Park?"

Assistant Manager: "No...[long pause]...but with all the forests and the river, Des Plains has more mosquitoes."

Estée: "Then you are telling me that Oak Park's mosquitoes come from Des Plains?" (With a slightly more-than-audible snicker from Estée.)

Assistant Manager: "Maybe, but probably not. I don't think they can fly that far."

Estée: "Then why am I paying for mosquito abatement from my Oak Park property taxes if there is no mosquito abatement program in Oak Park?"

Assistant Manager: "I didn't know that was on the property tax bill. You will have to take that up with the Cook County assessor."

Estée: "You have GOT to be kidding."

Estée called the Cook County Assessor's Office. The receptionist was too shocked to snicker at someone calling for an explanation of something on the bill other than the outrageous increase. When Estée finally got through to the assistant to the assistant manager in charge of bitching—sorry, customer service—she was told that the Des Plains Park District took care of that and she would have to call them. He had the phone number.

And so the circle was completed in less than four hours on the phone. Not bad as these circles tend to go. The end result was that this was going to be a good year for mosquitoes and a bad year for humans. It was also going to be a bad year for the few remaining crows that survived the previous years of the West Nile Virus, which had virtually wiped out all their fellow crows, along with the blue jays and a few other species of birds.

To say that Estée and I were sensitized to property taxes would be an understatement akin to anaphylactic shock after a bee sting. We kept after our ersatz architect in Ecuador to let us know what our property taxes were, first, on the unfinished house, then on the semi-finished house. His consistent comment was the infamous, "Don't worry about it." Finally, Diego, the son of the architect, took us up a mountain to transfer the title to us and to make sure those property taxes were paid up. We had plenty of money in our checking account in Gualaceo, so we thought we would be okay, but we needed to know the date the property taxes were due, so if we needed to transfer more money, we could get it done quickly. We drove up the nearly washed-out, deeply rutted, bolder-enhanced one-lane road in low four-wheel drive. The scenes of the mountains from our home in the San Francisco Valley at 7,500 ft. are special, but the scenes from the village of Cancai at a little over 10,000 ft. are spectacular.

It was a sunny day with sparse, lazy, white fluffy clouds moving slowly down the valley. The clerk in charge of the property taxes had to be summoned from a corn patch, and once he was officiously in place at his desk, he took our passports and slowly typed into the ancient computer. The printer came to life and started to spit out the page that contained the grand total of our property taxes. It was not itemized; there was simply a number. I felt that same twinge of tax anxiety that I had in Oak Park as I reached for the paper and gazed at the number. I turned to Diego, who was looking over my shoulder. He nodded his head. I turned to Estée and showed her the number. Our eyes met and a broad grin spread over both our faces simultaneously. The number was $12.97 per year, not per hour as they were in Oak Park. We could pay the tax bill anytime during the year. There was no due date as long as you paid the bill sometime during that year.

I could not help noticing that the Ecuadorian equivalent of the Cook County tax assessor was still staring at the computer screen. I did not like this at all. He looked up at Diego. There had been a mistake. I KNEW IT! It was too good to be true. My grin evaporated.

After a short discussion, Diego turned to Estée and me. We had overpaid our bill. The actual number was $12.17. It could not be corrected in the computer, or at least he did not know how to correct it in the computer. We told him to keep the extra eighty cents or credit it to our next year's tax bill. My grin cautiously returned. Estée poked me to whisper that I should keep quiet and stop whimpering in such a joyous manner. I could not stop. I wanted to dance all the way down the mountain, but I settled for driving.

Over the last few years, the taxes have gone up. We now pay $20.33 per year. Perhaps we are paying for mosquito abatement without knowing it. One thing we do know is that our property taxes are not paying for education, and herein lies a dilemma. Where does the money for education come from? Education is important in any country, but it is vital in a "third world" or developing country like Ecuador that aspires to be at least a "second world" or partially developed country. Currently in Ecuador, school is mandatory for children until the ninth grade.

School is free in state-owned and run institutions; however, fees and transportation are the responsibility of the family and those costs can ruin the family budget. No one seems to know how many kids actually go to school until the ninth grade. Only about ten percent of kids go on to high school. If a family moves from one school district to another, the ranking of the new school is not high on their list of things to scout out. The quality of the state schools is less than sterling.

If a family has means, and many families in Ecuador do have means, it is likely that the children will be enrolled in a private school. Private schools are very popular, and there is a certain prestige beyond a better education in having your kids enrolled in such a school. There is definitely a "my child goes to this private school, so there" syndrome. Perhaps that attitude is worldwide. There is the German school outside of Cuenca that was established by, you guessed it, Germans. There is also an American school and an Italian school. I assume that, like the Germans, the Americans and Italians thought their system of education was superior to any others and that, at some point, they had to share their superior system with poor countries. More than likely, some adventurous, or bored, or out-of-work teachers thought "what the hey?" and started a school for fun and profit. We have not found an Albanian school, but that does not mean there is no such school. There are also private schools run by nuns and priests associated with Catholic churches. All these schools are expensive by Ecuadorian standards, but enrollment remains high. This suggests that many Ecuadorians believe that education is important so their children might have a better life.

One such expensive but well-attended American school is in the metropolis of Guayaquil. I met one of the dedicated science teachers, an expat from

Atlanta, who came to Ecuador for all the right reasons. Mikie Emerson has the knack of being able to stimulate the curiosity of children and that, in the overall scheme of things, is one of the most critical components of education. Her classes started in the morning after the singing of the national anthem and the flag-kissing ceremony in which each child approaches the national flag of Ecuador to kiss the edge of it. The kissing is all done on the same spot of the flag. Imagine the lawsuits in the U.S. if that practice were instituted; forget all about prayer.

Not only would the constitutionality of such a practice be challenged, but kissing the flag in the same spot every day conjures up certain health risks as well; for example, the possible spread of the H_1N_1 virus that provided a health concern in Ecuador several months ago. Indeed, a case of H_1N_1 infection was reported in the very same American school, most likely spread by kids kissing the flag in the exact same spot, and the school was closed for a week. The parents were called and informed of the virus outbreak, which constituted one case, and were told to come to the school to pick up their children.

A level of panic spread through the parents as they descended upon the school to pickup little Juan or Maria. Most of the parents had paper masks to cover their mouths and noses; however, the Latin American cultural characteristic of kissing each other on each cheek took over, and the parents removed their masks to practice this endearing habit. The cheek kissing is endearing unless the spread of nasty viruses is related to the kisses. The tearful parents put their masks back on after kissing their friends and their children, swept their kids up in their arms, and quickly returned to their cars where, before getting in, they removed their masks and kissed their fellow parents one more time. Amazingly, the spread of the virus was minimal, and after a week, the school was back to normal and the flag was kissed each morning along with many cheeks.

With the quest of a better education and a better life for his children and the children of Gualaceo in mind, Pepe Portilla, the executive president of the orchid company Ecuagenera, decided that it was time to open a school. I know Pepe very well, and I know that he did this mostly with good intentions. He employs about seventy people and many of his employees have children. Many of these kids do not have good options when it comes to their education. Pepe's thought was to open a school near Ecuagenera's headquarters. It was a good thought. What could go wrong?

Pepe built the school buildings at a cost of well over $60,000. There is a large three-story building with a playground and a separate library. Pepe's wife, Ingrid, picked out the paint colors for the exterior and interior and selected all the furnishings of different-sized chairs and desks. They hired a school principle and started recruiting teachers. They named the school "The Bilingual School of the New World." That name was, perhaps, a little optimistic, but why not? Reach for the stars, and since Ecuagenera is at an altitude of 7,200 ft., the stars seem a little more reachable.

A lot of tourists came to Ecuagenera to go on orchid tours, and those tourists were shown the school and given a list of things that the school needed. Pepe is an incredibly charming person, so much so that Estée and I donated a $2,500 professional projector to the school. Never mind that it showed up in Pepe's living room showing movies to his family and, a year later, it was broken. People from around the world fell in love with the concept of helping. One person from Japan gave thousands of yen for band instruments. Another person from Australia gave thousands of Australian dollars for computers. People sent books from the U.K. and America. After all, the "bi" in bilingual referred to English. Someone actually provided twenty microscopes. The list goes on.

Dr. Alec Pridgeon was taken by the concept and mission of Pepe's school. Alec is a friend of Pepe's and wanted to help. One way to help was to "adopt" school kids, which, in this case, meant to pay for the costs of school, including tuition, uniforms, books, fees, and transportation if required. Alec adopted two kids from one family, which was a generous and noble thing to do. Alec is still supporting these kids as they weave their way through school.

Alec is one of the few true orchid experts in the world. He is based in Florida but spends considerable time in Kew Gardens near London where he works on all problems associated with orchids. So it was natural that Alec was tapped to organize and give the opening lecture at the First Andean Orchid Conference given at Ecuagenera.

Alec showed up a few days early and was invited to lunch by the family of the children he was supporting. He made arrangements to have lunch the day before the conference began. The family pulled out all the stops, and a fabulous array of traditional Ecuadorian dishes was served, including cuy, roast pork, fried plantains, corn, and of course, rice.

Included in the lunch, at absolutely no monetary cost to Alec, was some organism that everyone who lives in Ecuador is quite used to. However, it was an organism that Alec had not been introduced to at that time. It was an organism that brought poor Alec to his knees before the porcelain altar of his hotel bathroom. It was a difficult decision whether to sit or kneel since both were required, and sometimes at the same instant. A very weak Alec called Pepe to see if a doctor was available to provide some relief.

Pepe called Estée who was well known among tourists as someone who could provide commonsense measures during gastrointestinal crises. Estée drove the twenty minutes to Uzhupud, the hotel where Alec was staying, and administered ciprofloxin, which here is an over-the-counter antibiotic. A very weak but appreciative Alec showed up the next day to deliver the opening address at the orchid conference. Alec has been a friend, especially of Estée's, ever since—something akin to the thorn-in-the-paw syndrome.

Pepe not only solicited support in the form of band instruments, computers, books, microscopes, and money, he recruited people—especially from the United States, Canada, and Britain—who could help teach English, no previous experience required. People came with great enthusiasm and some were actually English teachers in their respective homelands. That enthusiasm melted over the course of several weeks to months.

It turned out that neither the Ecuadorian students nor the Ecuadorian teachers, shared the foreigners' enthusiasm for their perceived obtrusive presence on Ecuadorian soil. Some Ecuadorian teachers were downright hostile, perhaps due to their own inadequacies that might be exposed by comparison to a better-trained or more-enthusiastic teacher from abroad. Some foreigners lasted a frustrating year, but most quit after six months or less. Now, there are no foreign teachers.

Never mind the fact that there are few Ecuadorians to teach English; there is no one to teach music. The musical instruments are misnamed because these produce no music in the hands of the students of The Bilingual School of the New World. Without a music teacher, these musical instruments become instruments of torture that produce sounds that alone can only be described as noise pollution. However, when put together, these sounds produce a howling, screeching, thumping, and thudding cacophony that would, if the timing were right, accompany the rapture, the apocalypse, an eternity in hell, or whatever other gigs this group of children might line up. It truly is not the children's fault. There is simply no one to teach them music; but still, the sounds that emanate from those trumpets and trombones, those clarinets and saxophones, those bass and snare drums are spectacularly awful.

As the years have passed, fewer and fewer computers function and none are repaired or replaced. The microscopes sit idle near kids with no curiosity and no one to stimulate a sense of wonder in them. The dusty English books go untouched and no new books are coming in. Most of the time, the kids are listening to reggaetone, a more-aggressive version of what we know as reggae, or American or British rock blaring over the impressively loud sound system. Okay, it's better than their band, but still, I don't know how a teacher or a student could possibly concentrate on reading, writing, or arithmetic. That does not seem to matter because it appears that nearly all the girls spend most of their time in school preparing for beauty pageants. The boys spend much of their time learning how to escort the girls during their beauty pageants. People here are taken with the "Jon Benét Ramsey" syndrome. If their parents would only encourage them to learn the important things that would actually advance their lives…. Well, that might be said for many Oak Park parents too.

During the past few years, the enrollment dropped because it was recognized that the quality of the school was wanting. Kids who were able to transfer to the German school were set back a year or two so they could catch up academically with their peers. Pepe and Ingrid were fired from the administration of the school and now only rent the buildings out to the school with the constant threat that the school will pick up and leave to other facilities if the rent is not what the school wants to pay. Pepe's dreams of providing a quality education to his employee's children and poor kids in the area were dashed. But this, amazingly, did not detour Pepe's overall plans.

While the foreign teachers' enthusiasm waned, Pepe's enthusiasm waxed into the concept that he should start a university. After all, the school buildings that housed the grade school and high school were unoccupied after 2:30

p.m. when "education" came to a screeching halt with the last squawk of the clarinet. Pepe is a remarkable person and is enormously successful in growing and selling orchids; however, his Catholic education through grade school did not include educational theory, let alone the workings of a university. Starting a university is not a trivial thing. I was involved in starting a new Department of Medical Physics at Rush Medical College in Chicago, and the time and paperwork was daunting. I could not imagine what it would be like to start a whole university.

For Pepe, the solution was simple. Set up the university as an extension of an existing university, and there you have it—with little or no paperwork. So Pepe gathered three of his close friends to become the faculty of the University of Alfredo Perez Guerrero, Extension-Gualaceo, or UNAP, Ext-Gualaceo for a slightly shorter letterhead. The mother university was housed in Quito, and the president of the mother university was to preside over the opening ceremonies of the Extension-Gualaceo. Estée and I attended the grand opening. I was asked to wear my faculty plumage, which consisted of a black gown with gold panels and chevrons and a black and gold hood topped off with a black beret-style cap. Damn, even I was impressed as I stumbled my way to the stage to accept a calligraphy-engraved document stating that I was a proud founding member of UNAP, Ext-Gualaceo, never mind that my name was spelled incorrectly. I gave a speech of three minutes stating that Estée and I would support the university until our dying days, or the university's dying days, whichever came first. Few of the nearly 150 new students spoke English, so I had little fear that my feet would be held to the fire for such a promise. Most of the new students and adults in attendance had their mouths wide open since few, if any, had ever seen such plumage on a human.

Following the opening ceremony and a glass of some sort of nonalcoholic punch, the students were asked to go to classrooms, where a faculty member would give them an orientation. After I removed my plumage, I walked through a few classrooms where I saw eighteen- to twenty-five-year-old near adults stuffed into chairs meant for ten-year-olds. Over the next weeks and months, the chair situation was corrected.

The curriculum was centered on business. A few of the students were employees of Ecuagenera, so I could keep track of how things were going. It turned out that things deteriorated rapidly. Faculty showed up sporadically and student interest fell off quickly. It appeared that the opening ceremony was the pinnacle of UNAP, Ext-Gualaceo's history.

I was asked to attend some of the faculty meetings and after several meetings, I noticed that the chief financial officer was no longer attending. I asked Pepe if the CFO had left the university, and was informed that the CFO was caught embezzling funds from students' tuition. The sum was nearly $20,000, so we are talking about something greater than petty cash for a cup of Nescafé.

Months went by, and suddenly the CFO reappeared on the scene. When I quizzed Pepe, I was told that the CFO had promised to pay the embezzled funds back, so they took him back onto the faculty. No criminal charges were filed—sort of the "no blood, no foul" rule in sandlot football. I wanted to scream at Pepe, "Once an embezzler, always an embezzler!" I launched into a sermon on integrity and honesty, but after starting the sermon, I saw Pepe's eyes glaze over and I gave up. The CFO is still on the faculty. I don't know if he ever paid the money back, but even if he did, I would guess he is eyeing the university's safe as you read this.

After the second year, during which the enrollment continued to drop, the three good friends of Pepe who were the faculty members of UNAP, Ext-Gualaceo called a meeting in which they informed Pepe that his services were no longer needed at the university. It had become clear that he was not bringing any materials or money to the university as he had done for the grade school and high school. Once again, Pepe was fired and his dreams were dashed. The university moved to a building in downtown Gualaceo, so now there is only the grade and high school with declining enrollment in the extensive buildings near Ecuagenera. If things continue, all of Pepe's educational efforts will die out with the echo of a last squawk of a lonely clarinet.

Under the current government, there is an effort to evaluate and improve higher education. The sixty-one universities were ranked by curriculum, education of faculty, success of graduates, and facilities. Poor UNAP in Quito was ranked near the bottom. Poorer UNAP Ext-Gualaceo was ranked even lower. I can't imagine what was lower than that. This prompted the president of UNAP Ext-Gualaceo to resign. I think my promise to support the university until its or my demise is safe.

I am more familiar with what goes on in medical schools than in other departments of universities. Cuenca has three medical schools, although some would not regard the medical school at the Catholic University as a real medical school. It appears to teach from an advanced first aid curriculum or a remedial nursing course. The others, including the University of Cuenca and the University of Azuay, have curricula similar in titles to classes in the U.S. There are differences. For example, anatomy is taught in the U.S. by dissection, whereas in Ecuador, anatomy is studied from a book. The dictates of the Catholic church preclude the use of a dead body for purposes of, as the church preaches, mutilation. After all, you do not want to show up at the pearly gates in pieces. As for me, I think it would be best to show up a little disfigured so as to be less easily recognized.

Many medical school classes in Ecuador are taught from recent editions of U.S. textbooks, and exams include questions on advanced topics such as molecular biology and recent findings in genetics. I was impressed. I even heard the phrase "case-based learning." However, I discovered that a single faculty member taught the cases. Obviously, they had heard the phrase, but they did not know how to implement such learning.

Case-based learning requires the coordinated efforts of many faculty members who are expert in different aspects of a specific medical case. Teaching medical students using this method requires a large and dedicated faculty. The faculties of Ecuador's medical schools are made up of private practitioners who teach as a sideline or hobby. It looks great on one's resume to be a university professor. The medical schools do not have a permanent full-time faculty, and that is considerably less than ideal. The faculty is dedicated to earning money from their private practice.

Much of my understanding of the inner workings of medical schools in Cuenca comes from Nora, our "adopted" daughter who is now a sixth-year medical student at the University of Azuay. Nora accompanied Estée's mother to Ecuador almost three years ago. She was finishing her third year in medical school in Timisoara, Romania. After a month in Ecuador during her summer break, she returned to Romania to continue her training. I lost track of her for many months, then one day I received a sad email from Nora. She had dropped out of medical school and had become very depressed. The faculty in the Romanian medical school were extorting money and/or sex from the students to pass exams—a very nasty business. Nora thought it was better to get out than to put up with that professorial behavior. No kidding! I got angry just listening to Nora tell the story.

Over the course of a few weeks, Estée talked to Nora about the possibility of transferring to a medical school in Cuenca. Her parents agreed that this could work. After all, Nora was reasonably proficient in Spanish. Her proficiency was made easier by the fact that Romanian and Spanish are both romance languages and have remarkable similarities, especially to my untrained ear.

After arriving back in Cuenca, Nora and I paid a visit to Dr. Edgar Rodas, the dean of the medical school at the University of Azuay. In fact, Dr. Rodas was the principal founder of the medical school six years previously. Medical school in Ecuador is a six-year program and the first graduating class was to receive their diplomas a few days after our visit. Dr. Rodas, a native of Cuenca, was a surgeon for over twenty years in Miami, so he spoke perfect English, which was Nora's second language. Dr. Rodas wisely suggested that Nora backtrack a little and start the second year in the medical curriculum. Even at that, the adjustment was difficult. I cannot imagine studying medicine in a foreign language, let alone a third language.

The social adjustment was just as difficult. The class size was set at forty-five students. There was an entry exam of some sort, but selection of students was set by social status more than the outcome of the exam. If your parents were physicians and wanted you to be one too, then calls were made, pleas were plied, arms were bent, favors were called in, promises of future favors were made, and your precious but unmotivated and perhaps not very bright child found herself or himself in medical school. Ability and motivation came in a distant second or third in the selection process.

So Nora found herself in a second-year class of forty other students (five had dropped out by the second year) with a broad range of skills and desires. Since many had gotten into medical school through the back door, and since parental expectations were high, cheating did not seem out of the ordinary for many of the students.

Cheating can take on many guises and forms. Some are quite ingenious while others are rather pedestrian. Some of the more ingenious ways to cheat require modern electronic devices, for example the Blackberry or the iPhone. Some of the students took exams as if they were a contestant in a quiz show and could ask a member of the audience or even someone outside the classroom. They would carefully (to be undetected) text a colleague to ask for help answering a question. They would also photograph the exam for future reference using the camera feature on those magical phones. This reference library of exam questions and answers is similar to the extensive libraries that exist in fraternities and sororities throughout the university system in the United States. Some of Nora's Ecuadorian professors have caught on and collect cell phones at the door as the students enter the classroom for an exam. Most professors have not caught on.

The more pedestrian forms of cheating include sitting next to a colleague who you know studied more than you did and who is willing to share his or her knowledge. Professors look for this, and to the surprise of some who are blatant in their thirst for the knowledge of their neighbor, a big fat zero may be scribbled on their exam as the professor collects it partway through the hour. The consequences of too many of those zeros, or if one honestly does poorly in the exams, is the opportunity to go to *suplitorios*, or as I refer to it, supplemental school. This allows the underperforming student a last chance to pass the year and avoid having to repeat that course the next year as his or her colleagues proceed.

I asked my English professor friend at the University of Azuay, Lourdes Crespo, if cheating was rife in her classes and the classes of her fellow professors. I was assured that rife was a gross understatement. In the case of Ecuadorian students taking English as a second language, plagiarism was the most common form of cheating. The copy and paste commands on all types of computers are in full use in the English departments throughout Ecuador. To combat this form of cheating, Lourdes employs a computer program that matches the homework of her students with millions of written documents. Ah, the magic of computers, combatting the literary forces of evil with the literary forces of good, all electronically. Her computer program provides the percentage of a passage that has been copied and pasted, even if it is only some sentences. It also provides the source of the passage being plagiarized; very clever, this Lourdes Crespo. I have talked to several other professors, all of whom confirm that cheating is a consistent problem. It does seem that steps are underway to recognize and curb the problem to some degree.

I have painted a rather Jackson Pollock-like landscape of education in Ecuador, yet all is not quite so seemingly unorganized. I had the honor of meeting Dr. Gustavo Vega, the former director of the government agency called the National Council of Higher Education with the Spanish initials CONESUP, or the "can of soup" as I refer to it. With the help of Dr. Vega, a psychiatrist who practiced in Princess Margaret Hospital in Canada for seven years and spent a year as a visiting professor at Harvard, the evaluation and renovation of education in Ecuador is slowly being implemented.

CONESUP has recently morphed into SENESCYT, standing for Secretaría Nacional de Educación Superior, Ciencia, Tecnología y Innovación. Teachers in universities will be required to have a minimum of a master's degree in the field in which they teach. There are designated schools at which these degrees must be acquired. Teachers will not be able to purchase their degrees online. Research will be encouraged in all areas.

Another organization, with the acronym CEAACES, standing for Consejo de Evaluación, Acreditación y Aseguramiento de la Calidad de la Educación Superior del Ecuador, will, as the name implies, be in charge of evaluation, accreditation, and quality assurance of the educational process. Medical schools and law schools will be required to have sixty percent of their faculty fulltime employees of the university.

These changes are laudable, but I do wonder where the money will come from. Perhaps when I pay my next property tax bill, I will find out. Teachers in grade schools and high schools, as well as professors in the sixty-one universities throughout Ecuador, are kicking and screaming. It appears that reform will happen, and no cheating will be allowed.

Now if we can only get rid of those pesky mosquitos.

chapter 13

The Children of Ecuador and their Children: Who's Your Daddy?

The mostly white police car with red-and-blue trim slowed down and turned right off the road to Macas on its way east out of Gualaceo. It made its way at first almost vertically down the access road, then down at a gentler slope, trying to avoid the potholes and small- to medium-sized boulders. The quarter mile could take from three to eight minutes depending on when rain had last blessed the valley. In addition to the young Gualaceo police officer driving the car, there was a meek and sober thirty-one-year-old indigenous woman in the backseat. She was dressed in one of her best *polleras*, the colorful, heavily embroidered skirts that make the indigenous women stand out in a crowd. Her long black hair was in two braids that draped over her best almost-white blouse. In the passenger's seat next to the police officer was an envelope containing a legal document. On the front of the document was the name of our gardener of nearly seven years, Miguel.

The officer drove up to our gate and got out to ring the bell. The young woman stayed in the car. We do not open the gate, even for the police, if we do not know the purpose, so Estée went out to investigate. The officer asked if Miguel worked for us and if he was working today. The officer's black-mirrored sunglasses reflected Estée's expression of concern. Estée answered both questions with a "yes" and asked what the problem was. With Miguel, it could be any number of things. After Miguel was summoned, the officer produced the envelope and handed it to Miguel. Since Miguel cannot read or write, the officer explained the contents of the envelope. It was a legal summons to answer a charge of paternity. The thirty-one-year-old woman in the back seat of the police car was bringing a paternity suit against Miguel for fathering her child; well, one of her several children.

Once the gravity of the situation hit Miguel, he flew into a rage. The building of the rage took several minutes, since this type of gravity is not related to the physics type. But he finally got it and the rage commenced. Estée was able to convey to the police officer that it might be a good idea to stand a little closer to the back door of the police car to prevent any potential incident that could escalate the charges from paternity to homicide. He understood and moved to block the encounter. What appeared to be impending physical rage turned into verbal rage as Miguel vehemently denied that he knew the woman at all, let alone had any physical relationship with her that might lead to fatherhood. At least that is what I think he said, since my Spanish is less than perfect, or indeed, present at all.

Then the fun began. Miguel refused to take the document. He told the police officer that, in spite of his uniform, reflective sunglasses, and impressive car, he had no jurisdiction on the gringo's property. He was going to stay on the property and never leave; therefore, he could not be charged with a paternity suit. Estée had to step in and tell Miguel that, while it was an attractive concept, we, and the land we lived on, were indeed part of Ecuador. We, and our three acres, were not an independent country, we did not have our own flag, and we had no diplomatic immunity. In fact, we did not even have our own diplomat. I saw the look of defeat on Miguel's face as his hand slowly and ever so reluctantly took the envelope. He turned and walked into the casita. That was the last we saw of him that day.

Later that evening, Maria, our housekeeper and Miguel's common-law wife, came to our door in tears. Miguel had explained the situation. Then the truth, or the truth as she perceived it to be, started to tumble out of Maria's mouth. Miguel and Maria had met fifteen years ago in a town about ten kilometers south of Gualaceo called San Juan. There were rumors, and rumors of rumors, regarding the various relationships of brothers, sisters, first, second and third cousins, fathers with daughters, mothers with sons—the sordid list goes on.

It seemed to Maria that one little girl was around a lot. The little girl was about two years old at the time and there was the rumor that Miguel, the veritable Don Juan of San Juan, was her father. Maria rejected that notion at the time and rejected it again as she retold the story to us. The main defense suggesting to her that Miguel was not the father was that the girl did not look like Miguel.

I started to explain to Maria that genetics did not always work that way, but then I looked at Estée and gave up before she was on the floor laughing. Then I almost said that it was a very good thing the little girl did not look like Miguel and that perhaps there is a merciful God after all, but I ended up just leaving, which is usually the best course of action for me in these increasingly frequent situations.

In the days and weeks that followed, more verification of the rumors and the rumors of rumors came out. Denial slowly turned to *perhaps* and *maybe*, then to terms like *probably* and *likely*. Still there was doubt. We stayed out of this issue as much as possible, but of course, we still wanted Miguel to get a fair hearing. He hired a lawyer, one of the seemingly hundreds of lawyers in the little town of Gualaceo. Maria had to be with him, since he could not understand what was going on. They trundled off to Gualaceo and the lawyer's office on what came to be a three-times-a week trek.

On one particular occasion, the lawyer's office was filled to overflowing. Seated on one side of the room were women with children of various ages on their laps or sitting beside them. The other side of the room was filled with somber- to guilty-looking men holding envelopes embossed with legal emblems. The overflow spilled out into the street, where there were benches set up on the sidewalk. Remember, this is only one of many law offices in Gualaceo alone. It appears that there were very active relationships of the sexual nature that had been going on for a very long time. The immediate question that came to mind was "Why now?" Why were all these women seeking compensation and child support in paternity suits at this point in time?

The answer lies in a change in the Ecuadorian law. Up until a few months earlier, the government paid a stipend to the mother of a child of unknown male parentage. But recently, The Governmental Minister In Charge Of Formerly Paying The Stipend To Mothers Of Children Of Unknown Male

Parentage, or TGMCFPSMCUMP for short, openly told the moms of children with unknown fathers to go out into the world and find the fathers and sue them until they bled. Okay, perhaps there was no mention of bleeding, but that is not what the fathers or purported fathers thought. They definitely thought bleeding was in the new law.

This explained why there was a sudden interest by a large number of women to go father-hunting. It was all based on money. As I have often thought and said, when there is no apparent rhyme or reason for something, follow the money. It will almost always lead you to the answer. The mothers, however, were discovering that pinning down the exact father of any specific child was not as easy as they might have thought. By the way, few people actually use the acronym TGMCFPSMCUMP, but rather an acronym that is even shorter: SCREWED. Okay, it is not technically the right acronym, but both the mothers and the purported fathers knew exactly what it stood for.

As Estée and I mulled over the continuing saga, there were two obvious questions that sprung to mind. First, was Miguel really the father, and second, how old was Miguel's purported daughter now? The law stipulated that support was required until the child's eighteenth birthday, so if she were older than eighteen, Miguel might not have to pay child support. We brought these two questions up to Miguel, who had no clue to either answer, so off he and Maria went in quest of an answer to the second question at least. It turned out that the purported daughter was now sixteen years old. That would put Miguel on the hook for child support for less than two years unless the child went to school, in which case the obligation would continue for a while longer. Now to the all-important first question: was Miguel really the father? The judge had the same question, so he ordered a DNA test. The test cost $200 per person, and the girl and Miguel would have to be tested.

With the new law, DNA testing has become a thriving business opportunity and several new laboratories have sprung up in Cuenca alone. I can just imagine how many tests are being done in Quito and Guayaquil. The law stipulates that if the purported father really is the father, then he is liable for the costs of all the DNA tests. If he is found not to be the father, the accusing mother of the child has to foot the bill. This makes some sense and may avert a fishing expedition for unknown but possible fathers.

And now the story takes an abrupt left-hand turn. The mother of the purported daughter of Miguel refused to pay for any DNA tests no matter what the results might be. I am not a lawyer, but I think this refusal in front of the judge would be pure gold in a court. Any lawyer worth his/her salt would argue that without DNA proof of fatherhood, the paternity suit against Miguel should be dismissed out of hand. Not so. A social worker was assigned to the case to make an assessment of Miguel's assets. If his assets were above a threshold level, the court might rule in favor of a fishing expedition. The poor guy may still have to pay not only for the DNA tests, but for child support as well.

Now for that promised left-hand turn, and stay with me here. Miguel's purported sixteen-year-old daughter has a seven-month-old daughter herself. She, the sixteen-year-old, brought two separate paternity suits against two possible fathers. DNA tests revealed that neither of the boys/men was the father, so the sixteen-year-old's family was out a quick $600 to the DNA testing laboratories: $200 for each of the boys/men and $200 for the DNA of the child for comparison. The family did not have any money left in the DNA testing coffers as the game of "Who's Your Daddy" played out.

To complete the story of the extended family, it turns out that the mother, who is accusing Miguel of fatherhood, has two other children besides the sixteen-year-old daughter. The two separate fathers of the children have been positively identified through DNA testing, and so the two gentlemen are paying child support. I am all in favor of fathers paying child support, so when the judge decided that Miguel was rich enough to spring for the DNA testing, the mother decided that she was rich enough to get to the DNA testing laboratory in Cuenca on the appointed day. Sadly for Miguel and happily for the mother, Miguel's DNA test proved that he was the father.

After yet another trip to the courtroom in Gualaceo, the monthly fee for child support was set at $91.22. Don't ask. The money gets deposited into the mother's account, not the daughter's account, so it is really mother support and not child support. Miguel's first reaction was that he would not pay the money. The rule of the law is that you can get away without paying for two months, then you go to jail for one month. After that, you get another two months without paying, and so the cycle repeats itself. I would guess that the penalties get stiffer as time goes by. Some sense of reason hit Miguel and he made his first payment.

He is still contemplating running off, but we remind him that the long arm of the law is truly long, and he really cannot run or hide for two years until the girl turns eighteen. They will get him.

I have reflected on all the other mothers and possible fathers in all the law offices in Gualaceo and other small- to medium-sized towns and cities throughout Ecuador. It is difficult for me to get a handle on the numbers we are talking about. There appear to be many thousands of illegitimate children in Gualaceo alone. With the new laws that are designed to identify the fathers of these children, it would seem that a whole new set of business opportunities and marketing schemes might come to the foreground. The manufacture and sale of condoms comes to mind, with marketing strategies such as "Wrap that Rascal." Condoms are readily available in Ecuador even though it is a predominantly Catholic country. The Catholics actually get a bad rap for the previous nonsense that was promulgated by the Vatican regarding birth control. Thankfully, most Catholic people in Latin America ignored the nonsense and bought condoms anyway, except for much of Ecuador. Birth control pills are also available, as are morning-after pills, so apparently it comes down to education.

Many factors contribute to the number of illegitimate children in Ecuador, or indeed, in any country of the world. Among them: youth and the accompanying attitude that certainly nothing could happen after one night of teenaged passion. Other things that contribute include alcohol consumption, poor education, poverty, and a machismo attitude that puts girls and women beneath men (both figuratively and literally). Until some of these things change, the recurrent questions will always be on mothers' minds as they kiss their children goodnight. Who's your daddy? Who's your daddy? And, of course: how much money can I get?

chapter 14

Thirteen Ways to End Up in an Ecuadorian Jail: If You Think There Are Only Twelve, You're Probably Reading This from Jail

I t was late Sunday afternoon and the sun was setting behind the mountains, casting a magic bluish hue deep into the valleys surrounding Cuenca. The transit police buses were parked inconspicuously, almost camouflaged, around a corner next to the road carrying cars that were coming from the popular weekend getaway in Yunguilla, halfway between the coast and Cuenca. The newly purchased K-band portable radar system was proudly held by a member of the transit police, a recently formed group of elite police whose responsibility was to use the newly-purchased K-band portable-radar system to catch people going in excess of the forty-eight miles per hour speed limit on that section of the road and put them in jail. (The number forty-eight might seem strange, but it is equivalent to eighty kilometers per hour.) Yes, you read that right. Speeders in Ecuador do not pass "go" as in the game of Monopoly—they just go right to jail. It also costs one a $300 fine that must be paid before one's release. The "elite" part of the elite transit police is that you can't bribe your way out of either the fine or the three days in jail. The inability to bribe your way out of a jam is something quite new in Ecuador, and it has people up in arms, as much as you can be up in arms in jail.

The 2005 dark-blue Chevy Corsica rounded the corner where the K-band portable radar system was aimed and the reading flashed onto the screen. It was an ominous one-hundred-three kilometers per hour. Members of the elite transit police smiled as they waived the Chevy over to the side. A queasy feeling arose in the stomach of Jose Miguel as he slowed down and pulled off the road. The feeling was not quelled by the fact that an old rusty red Datsun was pulled over immediately after him. The two had been in some sort of competition for the last twenty-five miles. They had not really been racing, since neither car could reach a speed that would ever be called a racing speed, but there had been some degree of competition to be sure. Now, there was only remorse. The elite transit police in their elite black uniforms and their elite shiny black cars were happy. This would look very good on their records. As the sun set behind the mountains in the evening, the transit police called it a day, and the nearly full bus—the second one of the afternoon—pulled out to deposit the offenders into the local jail.

There are two types of prisons in Ecuador, one for the minor offenders like speeders, and one for the serious stuff like murder, rape, drug trafficking, bank robbing, and insulting any public servant no matter how arrogant, incompetent, or lazy he or she might be. Since politics are not part of this book, the reader must omit this last reason to go to jail from his/her mind.

I will not dwell on the more obvious reasons that can get one admitted into the prison system; however, there are some subtle ones that can get you into trouble with the law. For example, if you have a traffic accident and you do not flee the scene (barring a serious injury), you will go to jail until the police get things sorted out. Your car will also go to "jail," which is an impoundment facility, and if you are lucky, you will be out of jail before your car is out. It is no wonder there are so many lawyers in Ecuador.

Even though the jail in which speeding people are incarcerated is not the same jail where murderers and rapists are locked up, it can be a frightening experience if one is not used to it. I have not seen the inside of the traffic jail (yet) but a close friend of mine, Lourdes Crespo, has been a first-hand witness from the inside. To understand the degree of trauma that one might feel, you have to know Lourdes. She is an English professor at the University of Azuay and a true lady by anyone's definition. More than that, her family name is Crespo. There are streets, hotels, schools, and hospital suites named Crespo after numerous and famous family members. Books have been written by and about various Crespo family members. Small and large businesses are owned and run by Crespos. In other words, she is somebody. Twenty to thirty years ago, that might have meant something, but in the modern world, it does not mean squat to the transit police.

So when the transit police began waving Lourdes over to the side of the street in a sixty kilometers-per-hour zone, she quickly looked at the speedometer and sighed a sigh of relief. Her speed of sixty-five kilometers per hour fell within the ten kilometer per hour grace speed that was allowed, even by the modern-day transit police. Therefore, she was surprised to be told that she was going fifteen kilometers per hour over the speed limit. She would be hauled off to jail and fined $300. She was allowed to call someone to come and pick up her car. Her husband, Joe, was not home.

Friends and Joe, once he found out about the situation, pounced into action, brought her warm clothes, food, a toothbrush and toothpaste, snacks, books, and a lot of goodwill; all things a common criminal such as Lourdes needed. She was locked into a cell with iron bars along with other common criminal women who were being locked up for the same reason. There were tears from all the cellmates as the seconds, minutes, and hours ticked slowly by. Reading a book was out of the question as fights broke out in the cells down the hall occupied by the male counterparts of the common criminal women. The fights among the men were mostly a result of alcohol intoxication that had not had time to wear off.

Lourdes was positive that the sign on that stretch of the road said sixty kilometers per hour. She asked Joe to check. Sure enough, it was sixty kilometers per hour. So at the hearing before the traffic court judge the next day, an argument ensued. Lourdes, her family, and friends argued that she was not speeding (taking the grace speed into account) and the transit police argued that the sign clearly said fifty kilometers per hour. We all know that social media, including those pesky smartphones with their cameras, have changed the world, mostly for the worse, but sometimes for the better. This time, it was for the better. Family members and friends produced cell phone photo-evidence that the sign said sixty kilometers per hour.

The transit police were stunned. Even in the face of such evidence, they maintained their right to throw Lourdes and all her co-criminals in jail. The judge was not impressed with the transit police, which is pretty amazing since judges almost always side with the police, so she actually left her bench, drove to the scene, and discovered that Lourdes was correct. The charges were dropped and Lourdes and her co-criminals were released from jail. Of course, it really took another six hours to release them, partly because the person who had the keys to the cell was on an extended lunch/siesta break. But she got out of jail and did not have to pay the $300 fine.

How close have I come to getting hauled off to jail, you might be wondering? Not very close, but there was this one speeding incident a few years ago before the existence of the elite transit police. I had thankfully found the road that circumvented most of Guayaquil. Cars were passing me left, and yes, right as well. In the not-too-distant space in front of me, I saw a police officer waving. At first, I thought he was just being friendly, but that is rare in a police officer in the middle of a six-lane highway. Then I thought he must have been flagging down some speeder who was endangering the lives of us honest, law-abiding persons who drive within the speed limits. The third option was that he was actually waving at me and that he wanted to discuss something that was on his mind. It turned out to be the third option.

I pulled over and dutifully put on my safety blinkers. I thought he would be impressed. The officer was over six feet tall, very tall for an Ecuadorian. He wore a dark uniform and highly polished shoes that reflected the sun as he strode toward the driver's side of our car. He had the same type of reflective aviator sunglasses as the guard in the movie *Cool Hand Luke,* in which I got a good view of my worried face as I asked, "Hello, officer, what is the problem?" This was fairly early on in our retirement to Ecuador, so my Spanish was measured in a few words related to how one would offer a friendly greeting and ask where the bathroom was. The greeting might be all right in this situation, but the bathroom part was less likely to be appropriate. However, if things got really bad, the bathroom part might come into play.

Estée thought of a solution. She called our friend Pepe and explained the situation. She passed the phone to officer not-so-friendly, and as they were conversing, I noticed other officers waving cars to the side of the road both ahead of and behind me. The cars were there for only the time it took for the officer to stroll to the driver's side of the car, then the car drove off to rejoin the traffic that was consistently going at least ten to twenty miles per hour over the speed limit. I was curious.

After less than sixty seconds, the officer handed me the phone. I could hear the mirth in Pepe's voice. He said, "Just pay the officer $5. That is all he wants." I explained this to Estée, and we hurriedly went through our pockets, wallets, purse, emergency money we kept in the console, and the cup holder that doubled as a change receptacle. I even felt hopefully in the back of the seat to see if we could come up with $5. We could not. Pepe was still on the phone line as I handed the officer $10. I told Pepe we did not have $5, only ten. Pepe said without cracking up, "Ask for change." I actually did, but even the officer thought that was funny. He handed our papers through the window, and said in perfect English, "Don't speed, and have a nice day."

I felt slightly violated, only $5 worth, but as I slowly drove back into the speeding traffic, Nora, our Romanian "niece" who was in the backseat, suggested that if we get stopped again for speeding, we could simply tell the officer that his $5 bribe is in the pocket of officer not-so-friendly, the one that speaks perfect English. I am happy that the elite transit police were not in existence at that time. I might have been put into a bus and hauled off to jail.

It came to my attention recently that if, indeed, I did have a negative encounter with the elite transit police, and I was unfortunate enough to be speeding above the grace speed, I could have several days added to my incarceration owing to the fact that I did not have a valid Ecuadorian driver's license. This knowledge brought a bead of sweat to my brow. I had been driving for seven years on an international driver's license that I renewed each year when I was in Chicago. I was told that in Ecuador, the international driver's license was only valid for thirty days. If you were caught speeding and you did not have a valid Ecuadorian license, it would add six days to your jail term. Ouch!! It was time to get legal.

There are two options for expats to get a driver's license in Ecuador. One is to go to driver's school for nine days at a cost of about $180, and the other is to get your U.S. state driver's license "converted" into an Ecuadorian one. We opted for the conversion method since the nearest driving school was an hour away in Cuenca and we would have to make the two-hour round trip for at least nine days. We collected everything we needed for the simple conversion of our driver's licenses to legal Ecuadorian ones. This was not a simple list. It brought back memories of the list of things we needed to bring Pepper, our Doberman, to Ecuador.

Among the things we had to do was to get our blood drawn and typed. We also had to have our driver's license information translated into Spanish by an authorized translator and then notarized. Even the transit authorities thought the whole process was cumbersome and silly. The worst item for us was the need to take a psychosensomotormetric exam. Yes, I spelled it correctly. There was no appointment. We showed up at the third floor room-within-a-room to take the exam. After waiting a half hour, we saw the first person emerge. It was a young person, and there was a look of satisfaction on his face, so we assumed he passed. There was one more before us and he too seemed happy upon his exit so I thought, okay, if they can do it, so can I. Estée went first and after a few minutes, I heard laughter coming from the inner room. A half-hour went by, then another ten minutes went by. Finally, Estée came out to get me.

I met my examiner, who was a middle-aged woman who seemed pleasant, so I calmed down and took a fairly standard eye and ear test. Then came the psychosenso-part of the test. It was a game similar to one I had played when I was two or three years old, in which I had to put shapes into similarly shaped holes. Here, I had to quickly identify and match designated shapes on the computer. My examiner smiled as I struggled through that part. Then came the psychomotor part of the test. This exercise was to keep two little red balls within two white simulated lanes of two roads without running either ball into the green simulated pastures. Thankfully, the people who made up this exam omitted simulated houses, people, or pets from the simulated pastures. Hitting those could give one serious nightmares. The laughter I had heard when Estée was starting her exam had to do with her admission that neither of us played computer games. Again, my examiner was very kind and let me take my time. I passed. Amazingly, Estée, who uses the computer considerably less than I do, passed as well.

We proudly took our half-inch thick file with all our paperwork to the transit authorities. The transit lady in charge looked over the paperwork, and I could see a frown forming on her face. We were missing one key component. Never mind that the key component was not on the list of things that we were supposed to have. We pointed this out, but were told that the key component was on another list that we were not privy to. Getting that key component was not going to be easy. We had to have an Apostilled copy of a document from the Secretary of State of Illinois saying that we had a valid Illinois driver's license even though we were standing there in front of the Ecuadorian transit authorities with a valid Illinois driver's license gripped between thumb and first finger.

I had planned a trip to Chicago in a month, so I got the required document when I was there. I also got my Illinois driver's license renewed. The renewal process in Chicago went like this:

Examiner: "So you want to renew your driver's license?"

Answer: "Yes please."

Examiner: "Has any information changed from the information on your current license?"

Answer: "No."

Examiner: "Really? Your weight is the same?"

Answer: "Okay, I have gained a little."

Examiner: "No kidding! Give me a number. Are you a convicted felon? Have you been to prison? Do you take drugs? Do you use alcohol to the extent that it would impair your driving?"

Answer: "No."

Examiner: "No to which?"

Answer: "No to all."

Examiner: "Stick your head into that black box. Read line five. Do you see flashing light on both sides?"

Answer: "Yes."

Examiner: "You are good to go. Pay $5 at the cashier and have a good day."

It took a total of five minutes. For the first time since I left the U.S. I realized there were a few things besides family and friends that I missed.

I got back to Ecuador and off we went once again to the Ecuadorian transit authorities. Our file was over a half-inch thick with the new, but key, document I had obtained in Chicago. This time we had everything we needed; however, our psychosensomotormetric exam had expired. It was only good for 30 days and we had exceeded that by weeks. We would have to retake the exam.

We trudged back to the third floor and waited our turn to take the exam again. I was beginning to think we would be driving illegally in Ecuador for a long time to come. Again, Estée went in first. Both of us were hopeful that since we had already passed, the old exams could be re-stamped with the new date and we would be good to go just like I was in Chicago. Of course, this was not the case.

The usual thirty minutes went by then another ten minutes went by. I was getting nervous. After another ten minutes, I thought this was it. Getting our Ecuadorian driver's licenses was just not going to happen. The door to the inner room opened and a smiling Estée walked out. It took her a little longer this time, but her score was better. I also improved my score a little. If I took the exam another ten times, I might actually get good at it. We still had to take a multiple-choice exam of twenty questions, but we both passed that as well. We are both now proud possessors of valid Ecuadorian driver's licenses that ended up costing us about $75 each. It is not cheap driving in Ecuador, especially if you get caught speeding.

Going to even the less-serious side of prison in Ecuador is not a pleasant thing. We don't know that firsthand, but we really don't want to find out. I always keep that in mind as I slow down in traffic to obey the speed limit. In this case, prison really is a deterrent.

chapter 15

The "Beasts" of Ecuador:
Things to Hate and Things That Go Bump in the Night

It was a glorious, sunny, seven o'clock in the morning in Gualaceo with wisps of early-morning fog nestled in the mountain creases and crevasses, creating a mosaic of light-green, sun-drenched colors and dark gray-green shadows. I was wandering around the kitchen in my black robe and slippers with a cup of coffee, trying to wake up slowly to avoid going into shock. Miguel usually starts work by 8:30 a.m., and we have a little ritual in which either Estée or I ask him if he wants a cafesito, or little coffee. He always answers "muchas gracias, Doctor Ahmmm" or "Señora Ahmmm" because he still either does not know our names or cannot pronounce Estée or Wayne, both very foreign sounds in Spanish or Quechua.

On this particular morning, Miguel was nowhere to be seen. I wandered outside toward the casita where Miguel lives in the far west rooms on the ground floor. I was a bit taken aback when Miguel rounded the corner of the casita with a 16-gauge shotgun in hand, thankfully not pointed at me. When he came closer, I saw genuine fear in his eyes. I thought we might be under attack and here I was, caught in my black robe and slippers, sipping coffee. Before I could ask, Miguel told me there was a very bad bird in the area that had to be killed. Since he was speaking in an animated combination of Quechua and Spanish, I could really only guess at what he was saying. A better translation would have to wait for Estée. I had never seen or heard of such bad birds that had to be destroyed, beyond those in the Hitchcock thriller aptly named *The Birds*. I decided that pants and shirt were in order to hunt the really bad bird, so I returned to the house and to my closet to dress in my finest bird-hunting attire.

By this time, Estée was up and Maria had joined the small hunting party. Maria, with a similar look of fear in her eyes, confirmed the presence of the mal bird. She elaborated to tell us that if the bird stayed around, someone would die.

This was a similar superstition to the one suggesting that if you looked at a rainbow, you or someone close to you could die. If teenage girls were caught under a rainbow, they could become pregnant. A pregnant teenage girl who wanted to avoid divulging the real cause undoubtedly started this superstition. I wonder if she got away with it. Given the number of teenage pregnancies, we must have a lot of rainbows! We certainly did not want anyone to die, so we thought we should intervene.

Try as we could, no one could find the bad bird. After a half hour, we all gave up and started our daily routines. Miguel, still vigilant, was hacking away in the garden, Maria was washing dishes from the night before, and I was looking through the Ecuador bird identification book for a heading called Bad Birds. I asked Maria to look with me. She explained that the bird had very large eyes. I immediately turned to the owl section, and sure enough, the bad bird was quickly identified as an Andean Pigmy Owl, a small owl beautifully colored in shades of gold, tan, and brown. Maria and Miguel explained that this bird was actually a witch. "You see, witches can change themselves into any bird, but owls are their favorite," they explained. "If you see an owl and you cannot kill it or chase it away, someone nearby will be killed by the witch," they preached.

Estée and I tried to convince them that we actually wanted to attract all sorts of birds, including owls. We told them that owls were our friends, not witches. It was like telling a Baptist minister that the holy trinity did not exist, or that the rapture was totally made up to scare people into donating huge gobs of money to the church to save their sinful souls. Maria and Miguel looked at us like we were ignorant freaks from outer space. Beyond the obvious cultural differences that became startlingly clear at that moment, we realized that it was unlikely we were going to attract owls to our property, at least for very long.

On a different day, it was the same Miguel with the same shotgun who was stalking around the woodpile. Owls do not usually nest in woodpiles, so we wondered what witch-like creature we were hunting this time. We were told that there was a Zorro in the woodpile that had to be hunted down and killed like the vermin he or she was. With help from the dictionary, we discovered that a Zorro was a male fox and a Zorra was a female fox or a female prostitute. I guess it depends on the context because, like owls, female prostitutes rarely hang out in woodpiles out in the countryside near Gualaceo.

We certainly did not want Miguel to kill a fox or a prostitute that might be living in our woodpile. After many questions, gesticulations, and a bizarre attempt to draw woodland creatures, we arrived at the understanding that it was not a fox that was living in our woodpile, nor was it a prostitute, unless she was very small and covered in fur. It was a small black opossum. As with the owl, we tried to explain that we actually wanted the opossum to live a long, happy life in our woodpile and we wanted little opossums to frolic in and around the woodpile for generations to come—although now with two Dobermans roaming around the yard, that seemed unlikely.

Miguel informed us that the opossums were eating the passion fruit, so they would have to go. He liked to include the phrase "like it or not," but that conjured up the question "who was working for whom?" So this time he left the phrase out. It was a look of total confusion and utter incomprehension on Miguel's face when we told him that we did not care about the passion fruit. We were happy to share our passion fruit from our one-hundred-twenty-foot fence lined with passion fruit vines with a small black opossum if he or she would only stay.

To this day, we do not know the fate of the little Zorro, but there are signs that he/she, or his/her kin, may still be around. There are scratch marks on some of our tree trunks. It appears that a Zorro is climbing our trees in the evening, when the Dobermans are passed out on the couch, and eating the seeds out of the seedpods produced by these particular species of trees. We convinced Miguel that a cat is producing the scratch marks, and since Miguel likes cats, he is content for the time being to leave his shotgun in the corner of his room by his bed.

Superstitions and misinformation have lead to a large number of "beasts" raising their ugly heads. The widespread slaughter of all wildlife is one of those beasts. One of our biggest surprises after we arrived in the highlands of

Ecuador is the almost complete lack of wildlife beyond birds, beetles, spiders, and insects, and even some of these are disappearing with the rampant use of insecticides coupled with deforestation. We had more furry woodland urban and suburban creatures in our postage stamp–sized backyard in Oak Park than we have in and around Gualaceo. We live in the country, and you would think that there would be some furry creatures here, but sadly, they have been hunted down and killed, evidently to save the passion fruit crop. In Oak Park, we had an abundance of large, whitish opossums, rabbits, an occasional fox, and raccoons galore. Even a deer would get confused once in a while and wander down North Avenue until it got obliterated by traffic. Here, almost nothing. We have been told that a long time ago, rabbits, deer, and the spectacled or Andean bear were common, but no longer.

An acquaintance named Kyle was traveling through a town near El Pangui in the southeast of Ecuador called Gualaquiza. The tour bus he was traveling in stopped near the town center, and as he was stretching his legs, he happened to look up to a large open window on the second floor of a building where he saw pelts of a large number of spectacled bears and skins of boa constrictors. The hunting, killing, skinning, possession, and sale of these animals and their hides is highly illegal, so when the owner of these hides saw Kyle looking up at the contraband, she immediately closed the windows and drew curtains to hide any evidence that the government authorities might use against her.

She came down the stairs to the street level and tried to glean what Kyle had seen. Kyle told her that he had seen the bear hides and the snakeskins. He was curious how much tourists paid for these items. The going price for a bear hide was $75 and for a large boa constrictor skin, $45. Losing her fear of the authorities, of which she had little to start with, in favor of greed, she asked Kyle if he was interested in making a purchase. He asked if many tourists bought these items and learned that there was quite a market, both by Ecuadorians and foreign tourists.

Just like drugs or the sex trade, if there is a demand, there will be a supply. In this case, the supply is very sparse, and it is believed that, in spite of the government's best efforts, which are admittedly weak, the spectacled bear will be extinct in Ecuador in a short time. You could sense the feeling of sadness and frustration in Kyle as he related the story.

Pelts of spectacled bears and skins of boa constrictors are not the only sad wall ornaments seen in wealthy people's homes. Ocelots used to be quite common in the jungles of Ecuador, but no more. Ghosts of ocelots past in the form of hides adorn walls in wealthy Ecuadorian's homes, and at one time were exported to the United States, Europe, and Asia for fur coats and trinkets. The ocelots are disappearing quickly, partly because of the hunting practices of Ecuadorians and tourists, and partly because of deforestation. The United Nations estimates that somewhere between two and three percent of the rain forests of Ecuador, Peru, and Brazil are disappearing each year. These cats, along with jaguars, which are also native to Ecuador, need a lot of space. In our travels around Ecuador, Estée and I have seen sad ocelots pacing back and forth in small cages in what are called private zoos but are actually a series of poorly kept, broken-down kennels. It is so tempting to reach over and undo the latch to let the poor cats out. With my luck, I would get ripped to shreds as the less-than-euphoric kitty took out his or her frustrations for being cooped up for who knows how long.

On a memorable trip to the northeastern part of Ecuador, where ocelots are still reasonably plentiful, we anticipated seeing much more wildlife than existed around our new home. We were to get on a plane from Quito to Coca and take a boat on the Napo River, which is a main tributary of the mighty Amazon. This was going to be a real adventure. We were going to stay at a research station located in the heart of the oil reserves in Yasuní National Park. The research station was located in the territory of the Waorani tribe, which once again brought back memories of the brutal slaying of the missionaries over fifty years ago. I assumed that the Waorani who actually did the brutal slaying were long gone, and that their children and grandchildren did not practice the same brutal slaying practices. I dressed in my best adventure clothes, packed more camera equipment than a *National Geographic* expedition, and mentally prepared to board a rickety old biplane to fly the three hours to the real rain forest.

My first disappointment came as we walked toward a new Tame jet aircraft holding over one hundred people. The jet was packed full of cargo and people, few of whom were dressed in adventure clothes. Some even had suits or sport coats and ties, which destroyed any sense of roughing it in the jungle. We took off and headed east over the remainder of the spine of the Andes, and after twenty minutes of flying time, we started our descent. Where is the adventure in that? We landed in Coca and were met by a tourist bus that took us to a long, narrow boat moored on the Napo River.

I got some of my camera equipment ready to catch the wildlife lurking along the banks of the mighty Napo River. Nothing. We did see some oil rigs buried in the jungle not far from the river. There were flames dancing on the tops of the rigs with dark smoke dissipating into the dense, humid atmosphere. We spent two uncomfortable hours going east on the Napo before we reached a dock.

I unfolded my legs, which were numb from sitting on a wooden seat no more than ten inches above the floor of the small boat. We disembarked into a checkpoint that was very much like an airport security complex. I was looking for my TSA friends, but they were not to be seen. Our luggage was X-rayed and hand searched. My camera equipment was eyed suspiciously, but it was allowed through. I was expecting cavity searches. Why all the security? We were entering into an oil extraction field, and there had been a lot of trouble of late. All of our names had been given to the oil authorities long beforehand, and we did not look like troublemakers, so we were allowed to enter. A bus was at the checkpoint to drive us another hour and a half to the research station. This was our introduction to another "beast" of Ecuador, the wanton destruction of the environment.

The accommodations were sparse but more than adequate. We were to stay four days, and I was not disappointed by the opportunity to see some real wildlife. One of the first impressive animals to appear the first evening was a female tapir who tiptoed into the dining room—if indeed a 535 lb. adult female tapir can tiptoe. She looked like a giant gray pig on stilts with small eyes and a Jimmy Durante schnozzle for a nose. Not only did she enter the dining room, she also tiptoed up the stairs to the second floor to have a look around. The personnel at the research station told us that all we needed to do to be safe around the tapir was to stay out of her way. You really did not want to get caught in the stairwell with Tonya the tapir.

The next day, we were scheduled to take a boat down the Rumiyacu River. We were the second tour group to ever inhabit the research station. The first group had done their tour two weeks previously. We learned that during the boat trip the first group had gone on, the engine had conked out, and they had spent over eight hours drifting down the river before anyone discovered that they were missing and sent out help in the form of another boat to tow them back to the station. We were admittedly a little cocky since we thought that all the bugs had been worked out during the first group's trip. What could go wrong?

On that first day, nothing went wrong. We had a great trip with a knowledgeable guide who pointed out myriad birds and some playful monkeys. Now this was fun—and one of the major reasons we retired to Ecuador. We wanted more. The evening brought out Tonya the tapir again. We discovered that, while I am sure she liked us very much, the kitchen staff was feeding her tidbits from the leftovers. She knew exactly when dinner was over and voila, there she was.

After dinner, we were scheduled for a night walk with a Waorani guide, and with the promise of seeing frogs, insects, and things that go bump in the night. I was very happy to go. Estée was very smart to stay in the dormitory and read a book. The walk was to start from the research station's dormitory where we were sleeping and end back at the station in an hour and a half. We were told that the Waorani guides were famous for tracking and guiding people through the densest of jungles. After all, this was their home turf.

We got hopelessly lost in the first fifteen minutes. Over the next three-and-a-half hours, we wandered around the jungle like lost five-year-old children. The Waorani guide would emphatically point in one direction, and all seven of us who had chosen to go on the night walk from hell would charge after the guide, only to discover that we had already been in that direction—not once, but several times. Over time, my small flashlight gave up and I had to rely on others who had thought to bring extra batteries or a second flashlight. The "others" did not include the guide who now had to be guided.

When we left the research station, the generators that powered the lights, water pumps, and the air conditioners were going at full tilt, producing a homing beacon of noise. I noticed that the noise beacon was growing fainter and fainter as we were supposedly going back to the station. I pointed this out, but the Waorani guide gave me a look suggesting that a brutal slaying might be in the offing. I shuddered and shut up. After four hours, we came upon a road that over the next forty-five minutes led us back, tired and foot-sore, to the research station and bed. I did get some pictures of some of the most bizarre insects I had ever seen, but I also lost a little respect for the prowess of the great Waorani guides, not that I would ever say anything within their earshot.

The next morning, we split up; half our total group of twelve went bird watching, and the other six, including Estée and me, got back on the boat with another Waorani guide. With the memory of the first tour group's eight-hour adventure drifting on the river, off we went. What could go wrong?

We were nearly an hour into the boat trip when the engine shut off. Terry, a member of our group and an expert fisherman who is also knowledgeable about all things pertaining to outboard motors, laughed and addressed the worried look on my face. "It's fine," he said. "The guide is just changing the fuel tank." The tenseness in my face loosened and Estée released her grip on my arm. I watched as the fuel line was attached to the new tank. I also watched as the Waorani guide grabbed the handle on the starter rope and proceeded to rip it out of the motor casing. Terry was not watching these proceedings but saw a look of shock and foreboding reenter my face and saw Estée's renewed iron grip on my arm. He slowly looked around to see the guide standing dumbfounded next to the motor with the handle of the starter rope at shoulder height and the rest of the rope dangling down to his knee.

We continued to drift with the current and the boat headed toward shore. Thankfully, there was a flat place on shore to land the boat, and most of us got out of the way as Terry took charge. There was a small tool kit in the boat, but it was missing the one wrench we needed. Terry had a small knife and I had a Leatherman toolkit with a pliers. With these crude tools, Terry was able to get the screws out and remove the top of the motor casing. Now it was an easy task to tie a knot in the rope, thread it back on the starter sprocket, put the casing back on, and Bob's your uncle. BUT NO!

While Terry was fixing the rope, the Waorani guide decided that this was a perfect time to hone his mechanical skills and increase his knowledge of all things pertaining to outboard motors, so he reached into the starter mechanism and pulled at something. Everyone's attention was riveted to the proceedings, and in the blink of an eye, there was an audible "sprong" as a spring-like piece of metal sprang from the top of the engine. Time turned to slow motion, very slow motion, as the spring-like metal object arched into the air, not toward a landing place in the boat, not toward the shore, but straight out into the fast-moving, murky current of the Rumiyacu River, never to be seen again. The guide looked at Terry with a surprised and quizzical look, and shrugged while he said, "What the heck was that?" although he said it in Waorani so everyone could interpret his comment any way they wanted. There were also a few mut-terings in English from the passengers as well. Good taste prevents me from jotting these down.

After a quick inspection, Terry assured us that all was not lost. The metal object was the recoil spring, which meant that we would have to manually wind the rope onto the sprocket each time we wanted to start the engine. No wor-ries. According to Terry, it was unlikely that we would be stuck on the river for eight hours.

The engine started on the third try and off we went on down the river. Then the rains came. We were miles and hours away from the research station by now. We did a short trek to a saltlick, a place where animals came to ingest salt and minerals. Exactly how they know they need these salts and minerals, I don't know, but they do. There were no animals there to explain.

We also made a short stop at a lagoon where it was known by the Waorani that black caimans lived. The Waorani kept this secret since poaching of the black caiman was an increasing problem, and very few people knew of this spot. I think he was quite confident that we would never be able to find this place again, and he was right.

The boat started filling up with water and the river started to rise very quickly. Did these minor setbacks detour us from our adventure? Of course they did. We headed back, soaked and chilled to the bone toward the research station, Tonya the tapir, and some degree of comfort.

That afternoon, we were invited to a Waorani village, or what now passed as one. The village was much different after the oil companies decided in the early 1970s that because of OPEC and the surge in oil and gas prices, it was economical to wreak havoc on the Amazon basin and drill for oil. Texaco, now Chevron, moved drilling and extraction equipment to Ecuador, equipment that had been outlawed in the United States since it was prone to cause cata-strophic leaks. Who in Ecuador would know or care? The problem for Texaco at the time was to get long-term oil leases, which the Ecuadorian government was happy to give out for large sums of money; however, the Waorani tribe controlled the land. This was a problem for the oil executives since the Waorani did not drive cars or trucks; nor did they fly planes or produce plastics. They did not use oil products at all. As a result, they did not understand why people needed this black, foul-smelling goop. The oil executives, with the help of some Ecuadorians, convinced some of the indigenous Waorani that plane rides, hard candy, and sparkly trinkets were a fair trade for the rights to spill oil all over the Amazon basin, pollute the soil and the rivers, and increase the disease rates many-fold among the indigenous.

The equipment was installed and promptly produced catastrophic leaks, pollution, and diseases. I can just hear the oil executives: "Don't worry about it." Many members of the Waorani tribe bought into the scheme; however, there was a small group that thought that brutally slaying oil executives was the preferred mode of dealing with the offer. This small group has essentially disappeared into the rain forest. Once in a while, an oil worker is discovered looking like a porcupine with multiple spears sticking out of his brutally slain body.

The Waorani who invited us to the "modern" village put on a show of old-style dancing the way it used to be; however, they were mostly clothed now. Before the missionaries and the oilmen came, they wore no clothes. I sensed a level of discomfort as they danced in their spandex shorts and, for the women, halter-tops. An impressive Waorani warrior gave us an even more impressive blowgun demonstration on how to put a frog skin poison/curare-tipped dart into a very small target at a long distance. After the demonstrations in what would have been, in the distant past, a thriving thatched-roofed hut with wood slats for walls and a dirt floor, the Waorani went back to their cinder block homes with poured cement floors and corrugated fiberglass roofs, and cooked their meals on a gas range.

The kids and young teenagers, dressed in Nike, Adidas, and Columbia sports gear, played soccer under a huge steel roof on a cement floor. There were basketball hoops at each end. The teenagers were carrying cell phones, even though there was no phone signal anywhere near there. Most had cell phone shells that cost $3 or $4. It was vital that they had the appearance of owning a cell phone and they pretended to talk to someone. This is not unique to the Waorani, since we have seen faux phones and phone calls in Cuenca and Gualaceo as well. The pressure to "belong," even if you can't afford the real thing, is an extremely powerful force even in the remote rainforests of eastern Ecuador. It is the appearance that matters.

Oil has been, is, and will continue to be a real beast in Ecuador. Once a small portion of the catastrophic oil spills, both accidental and on purpose, was discovered, Chevron was sued for many billions of dollars. I received an email one day from a lawyer acquaintance in the United States whom I had met in Ecuador a year before. She asked why I had done such a dreadful thing. I quickly reviewed my distant and recent activities to glean which part of my behavior she might be talking about. It turns out that a Wayne Hanson had been indicted on charges of attempting to bribe the judge in the Ecuador vs. Chevron case. He was hired by Chevron and paid a lot of money for tampering in order to taint the proceedings. I was shocked but relieved that it was not something of a more personal nature, and assured my friend that I was not the person she had heard about. The case has now been settled in favor of Ecuador, but Chevron is appealing the decision, which could drag on for years.

That evening, we blew a farewell kiss to Tonya the tapir, had a fitful night's sleep in which I dreamt I was getting farther and farther away from the sounds of the generators, after which I was eaten by a black caiman who shared what was left of me with a huge tapir named Tonya who was hiding under my bed and went bump in the night. Dreams are funny that way. The next morning without explanation to Estée, I checked under the bed. Tonya had left the building. That day, we retraced our arrival steps. Our luggage was X-rayed again to make sure we were not taking out any oil, and we flew in the very modern jet back to Quito.

Back in Gualaceo, we were tired and ready for a good night's sleep. That was not to happen on this night. At 8:04 p.m., there was a loud explosion overhead, followed by another one two minutes later. Squire, our male Doberman who almost everyone is terrified of, ran for the relative safety of his crate. The two explosions were fireworks that marked the call to a party. The party was across the valley on the other side of the San Francisco River from our bedroom windows, a short way up the mountain. The location on the mountain along with the direction of the noise produced the perfect acoustics to ensure that the banks of six-foot speakers would not allow a second of peace or sleep. In one or two of the more than 425 articles in the new Ecuador Constitution, noise pollution in Ecuador is addressed, and these beastly noise-fests are not supposed to happen. But they do.

At this party, there was a master of ceremonies, and as we watched the clock ticking away the sleepless night, the specter of alcohol raised its ugly head, and the master of ceremonies became nearly incoherent by 3:45 a.m. The music, should one decide to call it that, is mostly reggaetone, which is a jumble of screeching instruments set to a thumping of bass produced electronically. The vast majority of Ecuadorians over the age of fifteen hate it, but if you are fifteen or younger, it appears that raggaetone is all you are allowed to listen to. I have seen cars in Cuenca that must be eighty-seven percent speakers. The trunk is a giant subwoofer. I have seen this in Chicago, too, so I am not picking on Cuencanos or Ecuadorians in general. The deafness rate is going to be spectacular in another ten to fifteen years.

At 4:43 a.m. (and yes, I am sure of the time) silence descended on the valley. We figured that the master of ceremonies inadvertently turned off the switch on the amplifier as his body slowly slumped to the ground to begin a several-day hangover. These are nights I hate, and the subwoofer really does go bump in the night. Sleep would have to wait for another time.

There are many beasts to hate, to be disgusted at, and to loathe in the world. Beyond the inane things we humans do to the environment with little to no knowledge of the consequences, it is what we do to each other that costs such a high price in human life that is one of the most appalling.

In a small village near Uzupud in the Paute valley, a funeral procession made slow progress from the Catholic Church down a steep slope, then to the left up an even steeper slope to the cemetery. The coffin contained the remains of a nineteen-year-old boy named Felipe, the youngest of seven children of Juan and his wife, Rosa. Juan was a day laborer on local construction sites, and Rosa raised the seemingly never-ending parade of children. The parents did not want Felipe to leave for Mexico to try to get to America, but he was determined, and with the promise of new income from his future job in the States, whatever that might be, they saved, sold land, borrowed, and scraped together the $10,000 required to send Felipe across the border with a coyote. Something went terribly wrong, and Felipe, along with three others, was abandoned in the desert south of the border between Mexico and the United States. Felipe died of exposure, and his desiccated body was discovered after four days and returned to Ecuador only through the extreme efforts of, and more money from, his parents and relatives, who had to pay all expenses. The $10,000 were gone forever. Today, his remains were being carried to the cemetery.

This is another one of Ecuador's beasts, the seemingly never-ending desire of many Ecuadorians to get to the United States. It is not the desire that is the beast, it is the process. The Ecuadorian parking valet attendants in front of the building where Estée had her business, and who parked our car on the infrequent times when we drove into the Loop in Chicago, were truly puzzled by why we were hell-bent on moving to Ecuador. They had spent a fortune and an enormous amount of time leaving Ecuador. They were legal now and very proud of it. I was going to a lot of time and some expense getting legal in Ecuador.

After the sad funeral, Estée was talking to our neighbor, Marina, who lives to the north of us, whose son had made it across the border into the United States. The family still owed the coyote money, and he had come after the family to get paid. Marina had to put the house in someone else's name to avoid having it taken away as payment for the coyote's services. Many people do make it across the border, but at great risk. Perhaps as the economies of the developed countries worsen and as Ecuador's economy improves, the real or perceived need to escape Ecuador will decrease. After all, there are so many things of beauty to love about Ecuador.

chapter 16

The Beauty of Ecuador:
Things to Love and Things That Still Go Bump
in the Night

One of my great pleasures in retirement is to wander aimlessly around our yard. Most of the time, our dogs accompany me with only slightly greater aim, which is to frolic and abuse each other. I was taking my almost-daily trek when my eye caught a flash of dazzling florescent green. It was instantly gone when I looked toward the bush where it came from, but there was rapid movement near a three-inch ball of gold-tipped red puff that constitutes the flower of the *Calliandra haematocephala* bush, or what I know as the red powder puff. The red puffballs produce a type of nectar that is a favorite of hummingbirds, and the hummingbird producing the rapid movement near this puffball was spectacular.

The fluorescent emerald green flash of sunlight reflecting from the throat of the black-tailed trainbearer hummingbird is shockingly beautiful. The black tail with green epaulets is over eight inches long, excessively long for the three-inch green body, and it flares out when the bird is confronted by other hummingbirds vying for the same nectar. The bill is less than an inch long and straight, which is significant because that dictates from which flowers it can drink nectar.

Birds in general and hummingbirds in particular are some of the incredible beauties of Ecuador. In the Midwest of the United States, there is the ruby throated hummingbird, and while it is beautiful in its own right, it would not make the finals of the Miss or Mr. Bird Universe Beauty Contest. Most of the contestants would come from Ecuador.

I packed up my fancy photography equipment and traveled to southern Ecuador to Podocarpus National Park to capture some of that beauty. Podocarpus, just south of Loja, is host to at least sixty-two species of hummingbirds, so I thought that capturing images of them would be easy enough. After signing into the park and paying our small fee, we parked the car and started unloading the photographic equipment. I began stalking about, looking for one of the sixty-two species of hummingbirds.

Minutes went by. Then an hour was gone. I saw no flashes of green. There were no flashings of blue, purple, red, or any other bright colors. There was no hummingbird to be seen. I was beginning to wonder about the veracity of the tourist material, touting sixty-two species of hummingbirds in Podocarpus National Park. After minutes, then hours went by, I started looking for birds such as the blue-whiskered tanager or the opal-rumped tanager. Even a dickcissel would do. After another hour went by, I started looking for a sparrow or essentially anything with feathers. I was not about to be defeated. After three patient days, I had a digital image residing within my camera of what I thought, on really close inspection, was part of an out-of-focus tail of a bird of some undetermined species. It was not a good outing.

The best chance of capturing an image of a hummingbird is on or near a feeder filled with sugar water. We have six such feeders near our house, and while it may be considered cheating in the bird photography world, I do have some fair-to-good images of the seven species of hummingbirds that can be coaxed to feed before the lens. These hummingbirds have names such as the purple-throated sunangel, the white-bellied woodstar, and the sparkling violetear, names that conjure up visions of beauty and grace. However, the giant hummingbird defies the image of a small delicate bird flitting about and darting into the throats of nectar-laden flowers to feed, then gracefully flitting on to the next flower, pausing for a second or two. The dullish-brown giant hummingbird flops about on its huge eight-inch wings and bludgeons the flowers into submission. So much for grace in the hummingbird world.

Photographing hummingbirds is a challenge, but photographing male humpback whales off the coast of Porto Lopez where the breeding grounds are alive with massive, highly excited males is nearly impossible. The expansive sea appeared calm when we had breakfast high on a bluff overlooking the small seaport town. The owner of the small resort where we were staying arranged for our whale-watching expedition, and presented us with a pill containing an unknown anti-seasickness medication that she assured us we would need. I took two.

We were picked up at 8:30 in the morning and driven to the dock where we boarded a small boat to take us to the waiting whales. To board the boat, we had to wade through twenty feet of shallow water with a silty, muddy bottom that oozed between our toes. Estée was certain there were sharks lurking in the muddy waters. The slight anxiety was worth a few beads of sweat, since to see a humpback whale up close and personal is a real thrill.

I prepared my camera with a lens that I thought would be perfect to capture an award-winning image of a huge male as it completely breached the water, then splashed with a less-than-graceful, water-shattering crash. I selected the wrong lens. Put another way, perhaps the correct lens was in the hands of a poor photographer. The male humpback did his job. He jumped at a forty-five-degree angle and cleared the water as he rotated onto his back. I caught the action out of the side of my eye, as my lens was pointed in a completely different direction. The deckhands took pity on me and pointed in the direction that the male would resurface. Together, we counted down the time to the next jump. There was no jump. Another minute passed and nothing happened. My hands got tired of holding the two-pound camera with the seven-pound lens, and I let it drop onto my knee for just a second. Anyone in the world could predict what would happen next. Just because I was not ready, the male jumped a little higher and a little farther. He stayed completely out of the water for an extra second or two. I could sense a degree of arrogance as he taunted me with his agility. I jerked the camera up and pushed the shutter button several times. The people on board with their point and shoot cameras were envious of my equipment, and comments were made that I must have gotten some fabulous shots. I pretended to be content.

After I got back home, I reviewed the images on a large computer screen and sure enough, far in the distance and out of focus is an image of a mammalian equivalent of Moby Dick, with his body completely out of the water, taunting me. I will try again someday, and next time, I will take three pills and use a different lens. Or maybe a point-and-shoot.

Beautiful places abound in Ecuador to the point that it is hard to know which way to go. One of our favorite tourist destinations in Ecuador is a place called Baños. There are many places called Baños, but this one is east of Ambato directly under the active volcano named Tungurahua. It is considered one of the most dangerous places on earth to rapidly drive past, let alone to live near. Estée's mother, Estera, was visiting, so we thought an adventure trip was in order.

The Pan-American Highway from Gualaceo to Ambato goes north up the spine of the Andes and includes some of the most breathtaking beauty in the world. The scenes one is confronted with on the road from Baños to Puyo are of even greater beauty. There are roaring waterfalls at almost every turn, waterfalls so intense that you can feel the power pounding on your body and reverberating through your chest. The mist created by the velocity of the water and the impact the falling water makes on the rocks and the river hundreds of feet below casts a mystical and riveting spell. I find it hard to tear myself away from magic and mystic places such as The Devil's Cauldron, one of the most spectacular waterfalls in the area and in the world. We stayed for several days in Baños and drank in the sights and the sounds. Thankfully, Mt. Tungurahua decided that she would spare us for the time being.

As our trip continued east, the altitude dropped to 1,200 feet, and the temperature warmed up. Our destination for this particular evening was Misahualli. We pulled into the town square and were immediately confronted with a gang of capuchin monkeys. A gang is the only way to describe them. They came into the town square every day from the surrounding jungles. The people in the town had been feeding them for years, and that helped put the town on the tourist maps. Estée's mom and I sat in the park in the town center and were immediately surrounded by monkeys trying to get into our pockets and fanny packs, which they had obviously seen before. They tried to steal our sunglasses and our hats, pretty much anything that was not firmly attached.

Their manual dexterity was amazing. I watched the dynamics between the local dogs and the monkeys. It was a microcosm of society. Some dogs had accepted the intrusion of the furry primates, while others simply had not, and could not accept the new reality. Some dogs played with the monkeys, while others whined, barked, snarled, and futilely chased the agile intruders. The entertainment value was very high for hours on end.

We crossed the Napo River to a resort, and after a good night's sleep, we boarded a small boat for a trip to an animal rescue center in the heart of the jungle. Our guide was a young German girl who had been at the rescue center for nearly two years. We caught her in her last week, when she was anxious to get back to Stuttgart and the comforts of home.

Many of the animals in the rescue center had been discovered by customs officials as part of the illegal animal trade. The animals were usually stuffed in boxes or suitcases, and if they were still alive at the time of their discovery, they were turned over to the rescue center. Other illegal animals had been turned in by owners who could no longer care for them. There were ocelots, acouchi, pacarana, jaguarundi, margays, and squirrel monkeys, along with snakes and birds of all descriptions.

The parrots were particularly fascinating. Some had been taught to repeat some words during their time in captivity. Those who could talk and those who were wild were kept together in a large net-covered enclosure. The parrots that could talk segregated themselves into one area of the enclosure and had nothing to do with the apparently inferior wild parrots, even though they were all the same species. I am assuming that the ones that could talk considered themselves the superior ones, but that may be my prejudice. The dynamics of these parrots would make a great subject for the study of animal behavior for a graduate student.

The next day, we found ourselves in Archidona, a small town with a zoo and a cave as tourist attractions. The zoo was a sad collection of small cages with hungry, poorly cared for animals, and the cave had neon arrows pointing at the entrance. Neither was appealing or tempting, so we found ourselves at a small *hostería*, hot and sweaty with not much on the agenda. A gregarious gentleman struck up a conversation, and after a half an hour, we discovered that he had a nature reserve outside of Archidona that covered 450 hectares, or about 1,125 acres—a not-so-trivial parcel of jungle. He invited us to visit the reserve the next day with him as guide. I asked him if he was a Waorani, but he appeared to have no sense of humor.

The next day we all went off on the trek and got twenty-eight feet on the trail when Estée's mom went down to the ground with a serious-sounding thump. I envisioned a broken hip or broken leg, a shattered patella, or internal injuries. As I approached, her body was heaving and it appeared she was having diffi-culty breathing. As I rolled her over, she had tears in her eyes, but her expres-sion was odd. She was laughing so hard she could hardly catch her breath. Estée accused her of acting as if she was taking a stroll on a Sunday afternoon in downtown Paris with a parasol in hand, looking up at the trees and the vistas toward the Grand Palais. That vision made her laugh even harder.

We parked her on a bench at the beginning of the trek, and Estée and I followed our guide cautiously down and down through truly wild jungle, past caves with worn floors, toward a rapidly flowing river. This area was inhabited many hundreds of years before the Incas, and I wondered what life must have been like.

We reached the river, and all around us were dozens of different species of butterflies. The colors were surreal. One had blue florescent patches on a black background with orange dots on the abdomen. This time, I had the right lens and the butterfly cooperated for a few seconds. There was another butterfly, a large one that was several inches high and stunningly beautiful, with yellow patches on black wings with deep crimson red bars on the abdomen. This beau-tiful creature would not cooperate. He (it was a male, I later found out) would alight near the river in a puddle, but when I tried to get closer than fifteen feet, he would flit off unphotographed and dance about, once again taunting me with the promise of a *National Geographic* moment. If I backed away from the little puddle that he seemed to be enamored with, he would return, just out of photo-reach, and land. I would snap away with little confidence that I was get-ting the photos I wanted, but it appeared that I would have to be satisfied with what he would allow.

As I approached to what appeared to be the limit to his comfort zone, I sud-denly noticed something peculiar. The butterfly was emitting a stream of fluid from the rear of its abdomen, not in one continuous stream, but in rapid pulses. I kept my distance, but now my finger pressed the shutter button with an increased sense of purpose. As if sensing the moment, the butterfly turned its back to me, and I caught the stream coming directly toward the camera lens. I dubbed it *The Pissing Butterfly*. I thought I had discovered something truly amazing. It turns out that this was a personal discovery, since this phenomenon is well-known. A little research revealed that this butterfly, and several others as well, are aptly called "puddlers." They siphon up fluid through their proboscis and rapidly filter out essential minerals before expelling the waste in pulsating abdominal convulsions. It is sort of pissing in some sense. I was thrilled, both by the beauty of the butterfly, and at the sense of my personal discovery of something new.

As we climbed the hundreds of stairs and forded the small streams on slippery logs on our way back toward the start of the trail and Estée's mom, we heard a strange sound. The sound was coming from the base of a tree that was about thirty feet away to our left. We were in the middle of a small clearing, so we could see fairly well, and what we saw was not anything we wanted to see. It was one of two things—either a large monitor lizard or a very large snake. From the size of the head, we all voted for monitor lizard because if it were a snake, the smallest one of us was in trouble.

I have been told that snakes and lizards are more afraid of us than we are of them. Whatever this was, it was not afraid of us. It started hissing and moving toward us. We never saw the body of this animal. He or she saw very little of us. None of us remember how far it was back to Estée's mom. We were there in a heartbeat. We rested for several minutes as we caught our breath. Whatever it was, it did not follow us. Once again, I got caught up on following butterflies and trying to get good photographs of them, but at night I still remember that beast, whatever it was, and occasionally I hear it go bump in the night.

When I returned home to Gualaceo and had the opportunity to view my photographic efforts, as meager as they were, on a large computer screen, I noticed the butterflies' eyes. They were incredibly beautiful and extremely varied. Some had bars and others had dots. One had a star pattern in the middle of its eye. Some butterfly eyes were bright green and others were black or brown with various patterns of lighter colors. I truly wonder why nature created such variations in butterfly eyes and if different species of butterflies see the world in different ways.

Ecuador is filled with unconquered beauty. The worst-case scenario for Ecuador's "beasts" is for wildlife slaughter, environmental destruction, oil pollution, and human trafficking to remain or increase in number, size, and ferocity, and for the beauty to succumb to the pressures of humans. The rainforests are quickly disappearing, along with the animals they support. The fish populations are decreasing off the coast from over fishing. Nearly all the native fish species in the Andean rivers have been destroyed by rainbow trout that were introduced almost one hundred years ago. Frog and toad species have become extinct from the trout's insatiable taste for frog and toad eggs and from habitat destruction. The colorful dresses of the indigenous populations are disappearing as each successive generation tries to fit in with the world as they understand it. The Waorani will be wearing Jhane Barns or Hugo Boss before long, especially if Chevron pays its bill. Change is inevitable; I know that, but let us hope that it is change we can live with, and that Ecuador's beauty will never fade away.

Epilogue

Thank you for sharing the trials and errors, the joys and successes, along with the gaffs and failures of our experiences retiring to Ecuador.

Estée and I remain very much in love and happy with each other, which is not always a given in retirement. After all, we are together almost all the time, and when you are not used to such proximity, which we were not, it can be unnerving at best and produce a war-like hostility at worse. We have adjusted quite well and have learned to give each other the space we need. Estée will have to write her own chapter to rebut that view, but unfortunately for her, there is no space left in this book.

Our house is ninety-four percent done. That might have to be good enough. We continue to have some frustrations, like when the cheap three-dollars-a-gallon varnish peeled off the wood on the outdoor window frames and doors within a few months of application. We paid sixty dollars a gallon for the best marine varnish available, so someone pocketed fifty-seven dollars for each gallon—not a bad profit margin. Separations are forming in the wood floors, doors, and windows, because the great maestro of woodwork used wet, uncured wood even though we were told it was dry. When rain is accompanied by a light breeze, we have to run around with rags to mop up under the windows, since slanted windowsills have yet to make their debut in Ecuador. Slowly, we are getting many of these problems solved. I am reminded by all my friends that these things happen in new construction, and I am adjusting to this too. We just completed a small project to add a patio in front of the guest-rooms. The project cost nearly double the original estimate and took four times longer than estimated to complete. We did not bat an eye. We are adjusting.

We sold our house in Oak Park after it was on the market for two and a half years. (See? I told you not to laugh.) We dropped the price four times. We did a lot of swearing at the bankers, none of whom have spent one day in jail yet. Why, you ask? Follow the money.

I continue to struggle with Spanish; however, I am improving. I understand many conversations, especially if they include words like "dog" or "cat," but I am still reluctant to jump in for fear of making mistakes. I am approaching the language from an academic point of view, which is probably a mistake. At least that's what everyone loves to tell me. Now, if Estée will just stop correcting me all the time…

Sadly, Pepper, our magnificent red Doberman and a truly great friend and companion, died at two-and-a half years old of acute lymphocytic leukemia. He is buried in the yard in which he never got to run. We think of him often and muse at how happy he would have been making new friends with the local pigs. Although no dog can take his place, we have another irreplaceable black-and-tan Doberman named Squire. We got him as an eight-week-old puppy from Guayaquil. He quickly became an ambassador for Dobermans. At first glance, most people are terrified of the breed, mainly from depictions of fierce Dobermans ripping people to shreds in movies. Squire has won over the hearts of many Ecuadorians.

A little over a year ago, another Doberman came into our home and hearts. We got a call from a veterinarian in Cuenca who said he understood we had a male Doberman and wanted to breed his female purebred Doberman. We could have the pick of the litter, and if she had five or more puppies, we could have two picks. We are a one-dog kind of family, so we were not very keen on having more. We agreed to breed our male to his female and thought we could work out the details later.

He brought Sabrina to our house in an SUV, and out jumped a friendly, outwardly happy but emaciated three-year-old Doberman. She was starving. You could put your fingers between her ribs. We asked the obvious question, "Why?" The vet explained that he kept her on his farm near Gualaceo and he bought food for her, but the housekeepers on his farm fed their own dogs and not Sabrina. He was not happy, but he had not solved the problem yet. The two dogs mated, and he took her back to the farm with the promise that he would solve the food issue. He didn't. Sabrina lost the puppies.

When she came into heat in about a year, he asked to breed her again. She showed up emaciated for the second time. We told him that the only way we would allow the two to mate was if we could keep her and feed her ourselves. He promised to buy the food, which he did. Sabrina became pregnant, and we were excited to become "grandparents" of baby Dobermans; however, she lost the puppies again. Tests were done and it was discovered that Sabrina could not have puppies. The owner lost all interest in her and was going to drop her off at the farm where she would likely starve to death. We asked if we could keep her, and he was more than happy to be rid of her.

You can no longer put your fingers between her ribs, and she does not snarl and show her teeth if you come near her when she eats. Now, she sniffs her food to be certain the rice with chicken is up to her new standards. She is our second great ambassador representing Dobermans. The two now-neutered dogs have a real love affair and truly frolic on the three acres of fenced-in land. One downside; evidently Sabrina survived on the farm by hunting lizards, frogs, or anything else she could forage. Beautiful small dark-blue lizards and several species of tree frogs live on our property, and she hunts them and eats them incessantly. We are working to break her of that habit.

Driving continues to be a great adventure and challenge, but we have avoided any serious accidents and have also avoided jail. Driver's education does not appear to have changed the degree of peril present on the roads and streets of Ecuador. The cost of owning and driving a car in Ecuador has continued to spiral upwards. The government has instituted a "green" tax, which is more a reflection of the color of money than any concern for the environment. But I am not mentioning politics. The roads in Ecuador are improving daily. There are fewer ravine-sized potholes in streets and fewer bus-sized boulders in the roads. A new law decreed that all the speed bumps had to be removed. Most of the authorized speed bumps were removed and the underlying pavement was smoothed out. People living near the previously official speed bumps started to put unofficial impromptu speed bumps in their place. Now, official speed bumps are back. The nearly invisible unauthorized speed bumps in the countryside still remain.

Cash and Pearl are still on the lam from the landlord they stiffed in Cuenca when they disappeared in the middle of the night. We inadvertently ran into them while shopping at a grocery store in Cuenca. Our meeting was frosty, and that was before they got the chance to recognize themselves in this book. I cannot imagine the reception we will get then. But since this book is not about conspiracy theories, or "those" and "them" who are all out to get "us," they will have little interest in reading it, which is good news for everyone. After all, I am sure that this book would be seen by all the Silverbottoms and the Goldfingers of the world as a great conspiracy, a giant cover-up—but of what? They would think of something, and the United States government would be involved and to blame in some way. Cash and Pearl moved in the opposite direction from where we are located. We are thankful. The Freeloaders are still freeloading. We see them once or twice a year at lunches. I am sure their grocery bill remains very low.

Expats continue to flood into Ecuador. Perhaps they believe that Ecuador will somehow survive the next great catastrophe in which the rest of the world will end. There was bad news for the believers who thought that the end of the Mayan calendar heralded the end of the world, except Ecuador of course. Recently, new fragments of the Mayan calendar have been unearthed. It appears that the calendar continues on, and now we see that the earth and humankind will continue on as well, at least for now. It was just a conspiracy. The bunkers in Vilcabamba and in the mountains surrounding Paute are available at bargain prices.

Maria and Miguel continue to work with us and we are very grateful for their help. Miguel had some new adventures, like the time he asked to go to town to get a part for his chainsaw. He did not come back for a week. His so-called "friends" talked him into having just one little drink. He was drunk for a week. He lost his cell phone, his best jacket, a belt, shoes, a shirt, and any dignity with which he started out the week. He sheepishly came back and we had the option of taking him back or not. We took him back, but only after Ingrid Portilla gave him a stern lecture on the evils of drinking and risking his job, let alone his life. He did not take his pills with him that help control his type II diabetes.

Unfortunately, he eventually got his chainsaw part, and on a Sunday morning while cutting a tree on his property, he slipped and fell backwards. He used the whirring chainsaw blade and his forearm to catch his balance, which is never a good way to catch your balance. It took thirty-eight stitches to close two wounds that were cut deep into his forearm. He is very fortunate to have all of his body parts still intact and functional. We suggested that he not wear his slippery leather-soled shoes while cutting trees, and Maria suggested that he not balance on a tree branch while using the chainsaw—both reasonable suggestions. After all, Miguel now has to pay child support, so more than a few people want him around and earning a salary, and more paternity suits lurk around many corners.

Sadly, Maria's mother passed. Her death certificate was finally signed. Her final age was stated as 99, but her real age at the time of her death was unknown.

Chuck and Karen left El Pangui and are back in Nebraska, their new paradise or utopia, depending on which one you talk to. Their Ecuadorian adventure is over. The last time I talked to Chuck in Ecuador, army ants were invading and he had just spent three days at war with them. It was raining and there were new leaks in the roof. Gordo, Chuck's contractor, successfully evaded Chuck, so he will never be forced to "make good" on his construction project. The Shuar gave up their housing development across the road from Chuck. Evidently, they got into a fight with each other and the partially built two-room houses have now been dismantled. We know of still another couple who discovered that Ecuador is not the place for them and are preparing to move back to the United States. This does not constitute a trend, but…Nebraska, along with most of the Midwest, recently suffered the third-coldest winter on record. I think Chuck misses Ecuador.

Sadly, but perhaps for the better, the University of Alfredo Perez Guerrero and its Extension-Gualaceo have been closed by the government. They did not meet the minimum requirements set forth by the governing bodies to qualify as a functioning university, or even an extension. I feel sorry for Pepe. He had a great idea—again. Even the high school and grade school has moved out of the Ecuagenera buildings. Again, a great idea, but…

Nora is completing her sixth year of the six-year medical program at the University of Azuay. She is becoming the star of her class, not just because she is a beautiful blonde girl, but also because she is studying hard, a concept that really needs to catch on in Ecuadorian universities. She married an Ecuadorian who was two years ahead of her in medical school. It looks like a good match.

The beasts and the beauty of Ecuador still abound. The beauties still out-number the beasts by far. More and different birds, butterflies, and bugs are coming to our property every week, and our dogs are leaving them alone (well, except for the poor lizards).

There is not a day that goes by that we do not look up into the mountains with awe. We love our new country. We will be outrageously happy here until the end of our lives, or until we get kicked out, whichever comes first.

About the Author

WAYNE ROBERT HANSON grew up in Iowa. After obtaining his PhD in Radiation Studies in the College of Medicine at the University of Iowa, Dr. Hanson did a three-year post-doctoral fellowship in Medicine and Biology at Argonne National Laboratory in Argonne, IL. Honoring his parents' repeated requests to finally get a job after thirteen years of study, he was hired by Rush-Presbyterian St. Luke's Medical Center in Chicago as an assistant professor and director of research in the Department of Radiation Oncology. He finished his professional career as professor and head of research in the Department of Radiation Oncology at Loyola University, Chicago.

Dr. Hanson served as president of the Illinois Division of the American Cancer Society and was awarded the National Medal of St. George in 2003. The author and his wife retired to Gualaceo, Ecuador in 2007. They relish their visits to the Chicago area to see their daughter, her husband, and their two grandchildren; however, they are guiltlessly happy to live in Ecuador. They are enjoying every minute of retirement, or at least fifty-nine seconds of every minute. All things considered, that's pretty good.

WEBSITE:

www.adventures-retiring-to-ecuador.com

FACEBOOK:

facebook.com/AdventuresRetiringToEcuador

Acknowledgments

I asked, with a little fear and much trepidation, for a few people to read part, or all, of this manuscript with a critical eye. The initial feedback I received was far too kind. My friend Larry Pelka thought I should be in touch with an agent after reading drafts of two chapters. While that made me feel great, I did not want to get overly confident; but Larry is a critical reader and he beats me regularly at tennis, so he is really not that good a friend. A true friend would let me win once in a while. At least I was encouraged. Carlos Sanchez does not have an attention span that would allow him to read a chapter all the way through at one sitting, so when he said it was great, he was referring to the first few sentences. Once again, I was skeptical. As you might guess, Carlos is one of my dear friends, so I can say that and get away with it. I hope.

Estée, my wife and best friend, had no qualms in saying, "This section is crap and here is why," and I greatly appreciated that. She helped me make the book better. I just wish she would confine those kinds of comments to the book. Graham Giles, a specialist in all things pertaining to education, was a critical reader of the chapter titled "Education in Ecuador: A Short Venture into the Unknown." He offered sound advice, and I ended up using most of his suggestions.

I was sufficiently encouraged by Larry, Carlos, Estée, Graham, and my good Ecuadorian friend and English professor, Lourdes Crespo, to plug on and continue revising. After drafts of several chapters were completed, my daughter, Sherry Haupt, became a great resource. She helped me revise the entire manuscript while juggling a job and two children. Sherry, your assistance was greatly appreciated.

Others who read all or sections of the manuscript and offered advice, corrections, and encouragement include Marti Sanchez and historian Dr. Mari

Firkarian, a Fulbright Scholar who studied in Bulgaria and visited the Andes in Ecuador for solitude to write one of her books. All made helpful suggestions which were either incorporated into the manuscript or completely ignored, but not without due and perhaps incorrect consideration.

I am especially grateful to Dr. Wellington Sandoval, former Minister of Health, former Minister of Defense, and former Ecuadorian Ambassador to Argentina, for telling me the story of the plane crash in the Ecuadorian jungle in which he was the sole survivor. This story has never been documented before and deserves a book of its own. He was very helpful in filling in details when I decided to include a brief description of his story in the chapter on healthcare in Ecuador.

Life in Ecuador has been a joy for Estée and me. The joy has come from friends like Pepe and Ingrid Portilla and their extended family. They have helped enormously with living life in our new homeland. Meeting Rosa Vintimilla and her sisters Berta, Patricia, and Laura was one of the greatest things that happened to us. They have included us as family members in fiestas, holidays, and weddings. They make us feel welcome in Ecuador.

A special thanks to all the staff of Windy City Publishers for their help in making this project come to fruition. Dawn McGarrahan Wiebe was my point person. I explained that this was my first time and asked her to be gentle. She was. Ruth Beach was my copy editor who was not quite so gentle, but I enjoyed the experience anyway. She did a great job pointing out inconsistencies, lack of story flow, poor sentence structure; all the things that good editors do. She was great. I accepted ninety-six percent of her suggestions. It was actually one hundred percent, but I don't want her head to swell. Windy City provided a great experience to the point that I just might do this again. My sincere thanks to all those who helped me in this enterprise. If it is not successful, it is clearly their fault, not mine.

Made in the USA
Middletown, DE
25 February 2016